Also by Andrew Hudson:
(co-authored with Roelf van Heerden)
*Four Ball One Tracer: Commanding
    Executive Outcomes in Angola and
    Sierra Leone*

Co-published in 2012 by:

Helion & Company Limited
26 Willow Road
Solihull
West Midlands
B91 1UE
England
Tel. 0121 705 3393
Fax 0121 711 4075
email: info@helion.co.uk
website: www.helion.co.uk

and

30° South Publishers (Pty) Ltd.
16 Ivy Road
Pinetown 3610
South Africa
Tel 011 760 2840
email: office@30degreessouth.co.za
website: www.30degreessouth.co.za

Designed & typeset by Kerrin Cocks
Cover design by Kerrin Cocks
Printed in the UK by Henry Ling Limited,
    Dorchester, Dorset and in South
    Africa by Pinetown Printers (Pty) Ltd,
    Pinetown, KwaZulu-Natal

ISBN 978-1-920143-65-7 (South Africa)
ISBN 978-1-907677-63-2 (UK)

British Library Cataloguing-in-
    Publication Data
A catalogue record for this book is
    available from the British Library

Front cover: Belgian paracommandos at
    Paulis during Operation Dragon Noir
    (photo courtesy of BMA)

CONTENTS

ABBREVIATIONS

ABAKO	*Alliance de Bakongo*, a separatist / federalist political party
ANC	*Armée Nationale Congolaise*, the Congolese National Army, successor to the FP
APL	Popular Liberation Army, the military wing of the National Liberation Committee
Avi / Avimil	*Aviation Militaire de le Force Publique*, aviation arm of the FP
BAF	Belgian Air Force
BALUBAKAT	*Association des Balubas du Katanga*, a federalist party based on the Baluba tribe in northern Katanga
BMA	Belgian Military Archives, Brussels
C-119	US military transport aircraft capable of carrying cargo, personnel and paratroopers
C-124	US heavy military transport aircraft capable of transporting 200 troops
C-130	US military transport aircraft capable of carrying cargo, 94 passengers or 64 paratroopers
CAMAC	Belgian military assistance mission to the Congo
Centres extracoutimiers	self-governing Congolese townships adjacent to the main towns in the Congo
CIA	Central Intelligence Agency
COMISH	US military assistance mission to the Congo
CONAKAT	*Confédération des Associations du Katanga*, a federalist political party with a political base among the Lunda tribe of South Katanga
DC-3 (C-47 'Dakota')	US propeller-driven aircraft with both military and civilian applications
DC-4	US four-engine propeller-driven aircraft with civilian and military (C-54 Skymaster) applications
DZ	drop zone
FATAC	Congolese Tactical Air Force
FN	7.62mm Belgian FN FAL (*Fabrique Nationale Fusil Automatique Léger*) rifle
Fouga Magister	French-built jet trainer aircraft
FP	*Force Publique*, the Belgian-led military force in the Congo from 1886 to independence in 1960
GR	Gurkha Regiment, one of the regiments of the Indian Brigade
Groupement	a military territorial designation in the Congo. English reference used is Command rather than Group
H-19	Sikorsky military helicopter
HQ	headquarters
Ilyushin Il-14	Soviet transport aircraft
JTF LEO	Joint Task Force LEO, a US military task force deployed to the Congo
Katangan	a citizen of Katanga in the Congo; also referred to as Katangese
MAG	7.62mm FN MAG (*Mitrailleuse d'Appui General*) general-purpose machine gun
MISTEBEL	Belgian Technical Mission to Katanga
MNC	*Mouvement National Congolaise*, a party in favour of a strong central government, led by Patrice Lumumba
MNC-Kalonji	*Mouvement National Congolaise–Kalonji,* a separatist / federalist political party based on the Baluba in South Kasai Province
NLC	National Liberation Committee, the loose political wing of the Simba rebels
NATO	North Atlantic Treaty Organization
NCO	non-commissioned officer
OAS	*Organisation de l'Armée Secrète*
OAU	Organization of African Unity
ONUC	*Organisation des Nations Unies au Congo*, United Nations Mission to the Congo, a force established to provide military assistance to the Republic of Congo
PSA	*Partie Solidaire Africain*, a separatist federalist political party in the Congo
Ratissage	a ritualistic revenge undertaken by Congolese that can be accompanied by cannibalism
S-55	Sikorsky (US) military helicopter
Sabena	The national airline of Belgium, 1923–2001
Sûreté	Belgian intelligence organization in the Congo
T-6	North American Aviation Texan ('Harvard'), a single-engine trainer aircraft, used in a light attack role in the Congo
T-28	North American Aviation ('Trojan') trainer aircraft, used in a light attack role
UN	United Nations
UNO	United Nations Organization
US	United States
USAF	United States Air Force
US EUCOM	US European Command
US STRICOM	US Strike Command
WIGMO	Western International Ground Maintenance Organization (The exact meaning is unclear, possibly derived from a combination of the initials of its CIA-financed founders, William Guest and George Monteiro. The CIA operation is said to have been named Operation Withrush

CHAPTER ONE:
BACKGROUND

In November 1908 King Leopold II of Belgium bequeathed the twelfth largest country in the world—the swath of land known as the Congo Free State—to the Belgian state. Over the next half century the Belgian Congo, as it became known, developed rapidly in the interests of the colonial power, to the extent that by 1960 the country and its inhabitants were widely regarded as having the highest standard of living in Africa. Why and how then was it possible that this enviable status was allowed to degenerate so quickly and so cruelly after independence?

The Belgian Congo, referred to as the Republic of the Congo after independence on 30 June 1960, lies astride the equator in the very heart of Africa. With a surface area of 2.3 million square kilometres and an equatorial climate, the country is 75 times the size of Belgium and almost half the size of Western Europe. In addition, it shares a border with nine different African neighbours. In the west, at the mouth of the Congo river, a narrow corridor of

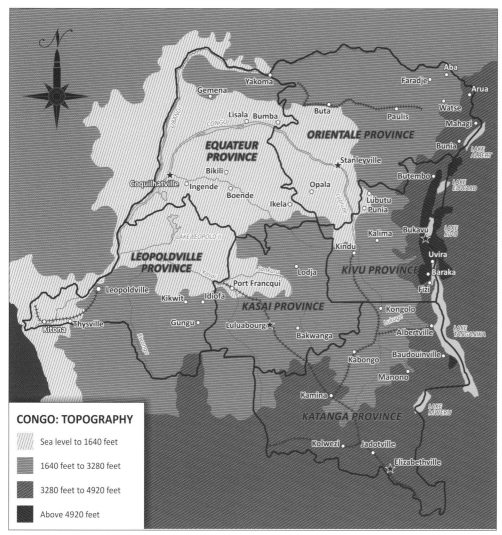

CONGO: TOPOGRAPHY

- Sea level to 1640 feet
- 1640 feet to 3280 feet
- 3280 feet to 4920 feet
- Above 4920 feet

Adapted from Merriam, A.P., *Congo: Background to Conflict*. Northwest University Press, 1961.

chain of five lakes, also known as the African Great Lakes, complements the eastern border area and stretches for approximately 1,600 kilometres, from Lake Albert in the north to Lake Tanganyika in the south. The southern and southwestern environs of the country are characterized by extensive plateaus and savannas while a trove of minerals including deposits of copper, gold, industrial and gem diamonds, cobalt, silver, zinc, manganese, tin, uranium, radium, bauxite, iron ore, oil and coal, make this region the country's richest source of export revenue.

Once the Belgian monarch had relinquished power over the Congo Free State, the Belgian parliament set about legislating its development in the interests of the mother country. Executive power over the colony was vested in the Belgian minister of colonial affairs, who delegated certain powers in turn to the governor-general, the highest representative of the Belgian colonial administration within the colony. The size of the country required that certain administrative powers were in turn delegated to the provincial governors of the six provinces, namely Leopoldville, Equateur, Orientale, Kivu, Katanga and Kasai. Each province was subdivided into a number of districts administered by district commissioners (23 in total throughout the country in 1956) and each district was divided into territories (132 in total throughout the country in 1956). A territorial administrator, assisted by assistant territorial administrators and territorial agents, managed each territory, which was further divided into chieftaincies and sectors (445 chieftaincies and 509 sectors in 1956), headed by territorial chiefs. On the same level, 39 self-governing African townships, known as *centres extracoutimiers*, were located adjacent to most large towns, in addition to 13 native cities. The Congolese communities on territorial level were largely self-governing, with their own courts, police, prisons and exchequers. Two judicial subsystems were established within the colony: a European court was located in each province, district and territory which co-existed in harmony with the indigenous courts, where traditional law was applied by traditional chiefs with limited judicial powers.

During the early decades of the colonial era, economic development was primarily directed towards the development of the mining industry in Kasai and Katanga, the two provinces located in the central and southeastern corner of the country respectively,

land allows access to a 40-kilometre-wide stretch of the Atlantic coastline. This tract of land is surrounded by the Angolan enclave of Cabinda in the north and Angola proper to the south. The remainder of the western border of the country is delineated by the Congo river and its main tributary, and shared with the former French Congo (Brazzaville). The Central African Republic and Sudan together form the Congo's northern neighbours, while Uganda, Rwanda, Burundi and the former Northern Rhodesia (Zambia) are located along the eastern border of the country. To the south Zambia and Angola together represent the remaining neighbouring states.

Blessed with an abundance of surface drainage in the central basin and vast tracts of low-lying equatorial rainforest sloping towards the Atlantic Ocean from the centre of the country, and with an average annual rainfall in excess of 1,000 millimetres, the mighty Congo river and its tributaries are central features of the topography, economy and everyday life of the country's inhabitants. This thick forest canopy gives way to grasslands in the north of the country; the eastern limits of this vast African territory are defined by the north–south axis of the East African Rift which separates the Congo and the Nile river basins. The terrain here is mountainous, with snow falling in the Ruwenzori mountains in the northeast of the country, at elevations reaching 16,000 feet. A

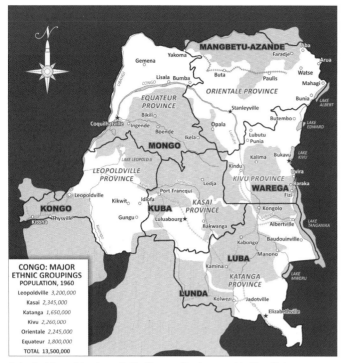

Adapted from Merriam, A.P., *Congo: Background to Conflict.* Northwest University Press, 1961.

Nurses at Union Minière, Katanga 1918.

and the transport infrastructure with which to support it. Kasai was the site of diamond production, while Katanga held a treasure house of minerals and is known to have mined the uranium used by the United States to produce the first atomic weapons in 1945. The backbone of the surface transportation system was based on the Congo river and its tributaries, of which approximately 14,000 kilometres were navigable all year round; an integrated system, which combined road, rail and river-barge transport between destinations, became a feature thereof throughout the country. After the Second World War the colonial authorities also embarked on an ambitious endeavour to facilitate the air transportation of passengers throughout the country and by independence the Belgian Congo boasted a total of 107 airfields and airports. Sabena, the Belgian national airline, established an extensive internal passenger air service using DC-3s. The relatively rapid movement of large numbers of passengers and military forces to the far reaches of the country became a reality.

The colonial administration also developed and reorganized the agricultural sector throughout the country where it was viable, resulting in substantial increases in the exported volumes of timber, quinine, sisal, sugar, beef, citrus, palm oil, latex, cotton, coffee and groundnuts to Belgium. The decade before independence also saw the colonial authority embark on an ambitious programme of economic and social development with the emphasis on housing, energy supply and healthcare infrastructure. Healthcare and education services were state-controlled but were developed and run primarily by the 730-odd Roman Catholic and Protestant missions and churches, subsidized church schools and clinics located throughout the country. Under the direction of the chief medical officer 339 hospitals, 1,642 rural and 192 special medical facilities with a total of approximately 65,000 beds were available by 1956. In addition, by 1954 as many as 37% of Congolese

children between the ages of six and fourteen were at school, a feat unmatched in the rest of Africa. The University of Lovanium, Leopoldville and a university at Elisabethville had been established but fewer than 20 Congolese had graduated by 1960 with no Congolese educated in the disciplines required of high political office. Similarly the number of Congolese employed in the upper echelons in the civil service was negligible, with only three of the top 1,400 civil service posts filled by Congolese.

By independence in 1960, 77% of the approximately 13.6 million Congolese, from more than 200 different African tribes, and approximately 125,000 Europeans, still lived in the rural areas of the country. The more important cultural clusters, within which the various tribes were grouped, included the Kongo, Mongo, Kuba, Lunda, Luba, Warenga and the Mangbetu-Azande. The Kongo Kingdom, at its zenith in the seventeenth century, was located in the southwest of the country and its boundaries extended into Angola, Cabinda and the French Congo. Joseph Kasavubu, the first president of the independent Republic of the Congo, was born and educated in this cluster and based many of his political claims and philosophies of ethnic separatism on his Kongo origins. The Mongo, with a population of approximately 2 million people, inhabited the central area of the country, while the Kuba people hailed from Kasai and numbered approximately 120,000. The Lunda cultural cluster, together with related peoples, occupied most of the eastern half of Angola, as well as smaller areas inside Northern Rhodesia and the Congo and consisted of three groups: the Northern Lunda in the Kasai province, the Eastern group mostly in Northern Rhodesia and the Southern group located primarily in the Congo's Katanga province. Moise Tshombe, the future prime minister of the Congo hailed from this cluster. The Luba people, numbering approximately 1,400,000 at independence, occupied the northern areas of Katanga province and southeastern Kasai province. Albert Kalonji, who led the secession of Southern Kasai, was a member of this cluster. The Warenga group in the eastern Congo occupied the hilly, rainforest area and was composed of members from the Warenga and the Bemba tribes as well as elements of the Songolo, Zemba, Bongo-bongo, Babuye and Taku tribes. Finally, the Mangbetu-Azande group, found in the northern Congo and neighbouring Sudan, are thought to have developed from Sudanese invaders who reached the area in the sixteenth century. While these cultural clusters were undoubtedly dominant within their resident areas, there was no single dominant group within the country as a whole. A further characteristic of the widely dispersed and distributed peoples of the Congo was the fact that the development of political parties tended to coincide with ethnic and tribal affiliations. Traditional tribal conflict was commonplace within the Congo long before the arrival of the Belgians, but it was put down forcibly thereafter. Once the colonial power began to relinquish its tight hold over the country as independence approached, old tribal and ethnic tensions resurfaced and, coupled to the lack of coincidence between ethnic and administrative boundaries, led to political and ethnic conflicts which were exacerbated by the social and political differences between rural and urban inhabitants. It would, therefore, have been no small feat for any fledgling Congolese political party or coalition of parties to rule such a country within a unitary-type political dispensation.

Of the nine countries surrounding the Congo in 1960 the majority could be regarded as devoid of any military or political threat against the interests of the Congo and Belgium itself. The political winds of Pan-Africanism, nationalism and anti-colonialism had indeed been felt throughout the region which affected the Congo and its neighbours in different ways. Angola was still a Portuguese overseas province and the Portuguese Armed Forces (Belgium's NATO allies) stationed in the country harboured no malice towards, or territorial interest in, their northern neighbour. By 1961, however, an insurgency in Angola saw the southern parts of the Congo increase in volatility as Angolan insurgent groups utilized this area as an external base. Northern Rhodesia, on the Congo's southeastern border, was itself experiencing pressure from both the United Nations and the Organization of African Unity to decolonize; the Federation of Rhodesia and Nyasaland to which it belonged ceased to exist on 31 December 1963. Northern Rhodesia gained independence from the United Kingdom as the new nation of Zambia in October the following year. On the eastern border of the country, Tanganyika was, by Congolese independence, self-absorbed in its own quest for independence and self-definition and presented no direct threat. It was only later in the 1960s, however, that the former British colony lent both political, material and logistic support across Lake Tanganyika to the rebel forces opposed to the Congolese government. Uganda, also on the eastern border, gained its independence from Britain in 1962 and followed a similar course of action as Tanganyika towards the Congo. Ruanda-Urundi, a Belgian mandate territory, was

the scene of tribal tensions between the Tutsi and Hutu groups, which culminated in the 1959 Rwandan revolution and the exile of more than 100,000 Tutsis to neighbouring countries, including the Congo. Rwanda was separated from Burundi and both countries were granted independence in July 1962. Burundi's independence was influenced to some extent by the instability and ethnic persecution that occurred in Rwanda. Regarding Sudan, on the northern frontier of the Congo, the British colonial power followed a policy of running this large country as two separate territories, the north (Muslim) and south (Christian) and, in 1955, the year before independence, an 18-year-long civil war between northern and southern Sudan broke out. In spite of this internal instability the Sudan allied itself with the Pan-Africanist and anti-colonial movements, extending both political and material support to the rebel movements in the Congo. The Central African Republic gained its independence from France in August 1960 and the subsequent political instability in the country led to the declaration of a one-party state and the ascent of Colonel (later Emperor) Jean-Bédel Bokassa in a coup d'état. Finally, the Republic of the Congo (Brazzaville), Congo Leopoldville's western neighbour, was granted full independence from France in August 1960. The country was wracked by political instability and military rule thereafter and in 1965 aligned itself with the Soviet Union, the People's Republic of China, North Korea and North Vietnam. In essence, therefore, while there was very little in the way of a direct external threat to the Congo's territorial integrity in the early 1960s, the political instability in the neighbouring states and the interests of the Cold War participants in the region tended to accentuate and exacerbate the underlying divisions and conflict potential within the country.

Internationally the United States government's interest in a stable, evolutionary Congo, within the control of its Belgian ally was expressed thus in 1954: "... the United States is vitally interested in the continual flow of mineral products from this area; that any interruption in this flow, whether in consequence of an economic crisis or political factors, was of paramount importance."[1] On the other hand, the Soviet Union's capability to project its military power and intervene decisively in the Congo was limited at this point despite the opportunities that arose out of the precipitous end to the Belgian Congo. Cold War rivalry was, however, destined to play a pivotal role in the affairs of the Congo in the decades ahead.

The Congo's greatest challenges at independence and thereafter were its natural, physical and ethnic diversity, its size and the lack of any political impetus on the part of the colonial power or the indigenous politicians to rise above narrow self-interest and overcome the centripetal forces which had the potential to render the country asunder. Internationally, the strategic location and roiling Cold War interests in Africa militated against any possibility of a peaceful future.

---

[1]   US Foreign Relations, 1952–1954, Vol XI, *Belgian Congo: Matters of Concern to the United States in the Belgian Congo*, 511.55a/2-354, pp 416.

CHAPTER TWO:
MILITARY FORCES IN THE BELGIAN CONGO AT INDEPENDENCE, 1960

Force Publique parade at Irebu on the Congo river, 1910.
Source: A Hudson collection

Two military organizations were active within the Belgian Congo at independence: an indigenous force known as the *Force Publique* (FP) or the army, and individuals and units from the Belgian armed forces who served on a rotation basis.

The *Force Publique* (FP)

The FP was created by a royal decree issued by King Leopold II in August 1888 with a view to providing a local militia force as well as a gendarmerie, or armed police force, in the Congo Free State. The force, which could be described as a colonial army, consisted of companies of ethnically mixed, levied and conscripted African men, some from as far away as Zanzibar and West Africa, commanded by European officers and non-commissioned officers (NCOs). The measures they employed to control the Congolese peoples throughout the country ultimately produced relative stability, interspersed with sporadic mutinous actions.

With the advent of the Belgian Congo in 1908, the FP increased in strength to 12,000 men, organized into 21 separate field companies, six training units and an artillery and engineer unit. Each field company was designed to consist of four Belgian officers and NCOs, and up to 150 men organized in 50-man platoons. By 1914 the FP numbered about 17,000 men, with 178 mostly Belgian officers and 235 mostly Belgian NCOs, the majority of whom served primarily in a police role in small static garrisons distributed throughout the country. The men enlisted for a period of seven years, carried single-shot 11mm Albini rifles and were supported by Maxim machine guns, and Nordenfelt 4.7cm and Krupp 7.5cm guns. The artillery and engineer unit manned 160mm guns that were deployed in static positions at Fort Boma on the Congo river mouth.

During the early years of the First World War the absence of conventional warfare skills and operational experience above company level only enabled the FP to assume a defensive posture against German forces in German East Africa (later

Tanganyika). This changed over time and the FP, a force of three brigades consisting of 15 battalions, was successfully engaged in conventional operations against German colonial forces in the Cameroons, Ruanda-Urundi and German East Africa.

In 1919 the defined mission of the FP in the Belgian Congo included the occupation and defence of the Congo colony, the maintenance of public order, the prevention of insurrection and the assurance of the execution of laws, decrees, ordinances and rules. The lessons learned during the First World War also prompted the colonial administration to reorganize the FP along lines which would improve its ability to fulfil the dual missions of external defence and internal security. The FP was then split into garrison troops, consisting of military forces earmarked to counter external threats, and territorial service troops whose role was to carry out policing or gendarmerie duties. The commander of the FP retained command over both arms of the force; it was foreseen that police troops would rotate periodically with garrison soldiers to ensure cross-training. This reorganization, however, did not necessarily improve professional competence during the inter-war years and the standard of the territorial service troops deteriorated to the extent that they were regarded as being incapable of conducting serious operations, or of even coping with local riots. Local administrators were forced to use Garrison troops to provide internal security as a result and a 1946 commission found itself facing the same concerns that had plagued the force prior to the First World War.

During the Second World War the FP provided more than three brigades with which to conduct operations against German and Italian forces during the East Africa campaign and in the Middle East. Despite the fact that Belgium had surrendered to Germany on 28 May 1940 and the country had been occupied by German forces, the FP, under the auspices of the Free Belgian Forces contributed to the Allied war effort with its numbers growing to 40,000 in three brigades, a river force and support units. FP units saw action as part of the British forces in Anglo-Egyptian Sudan and during the Allied campaign in Abyssinia (Ethiopia). Troops also assisted in the establishment of an overland route from Lagos, in Nigeria, through the Sudan to Cairo and 9,000 members of the FP expeditionary force served in Egypt and Palestine. Congolese and Belgian medical station staff also served with British medical services in Abyssinia, Somalia, Madagascar and Burma.

After the Second World War the FP reverted to its dual role of maintaining public order while ensuring the territorial integrity of the Belgian Congo. Mindful of the latent danger of inter-tribal conflict, jealousy and simmering traditional tensions between the various tribes within the country the leadership cadre of the FP was careful to ensure that the composition of FP units did not necessarily reflect a predominance of any specific tribe; the

Force Publique infantryman.
Source: J.P. Sonck collection

King Badouin visits the Force Publique (FP) school at Luluabourg, 1955.

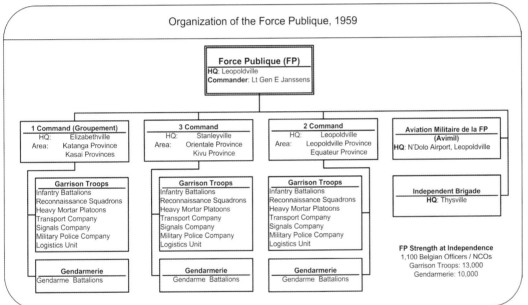

Organization of the Force Publique, 1959

Force Publique (FP)
HQ: Leopoldville
Commander: Lt Gen E Janssens

1 Command (Groupement)
HQ: Elizabethville
Area: Katanga Province
Kasai Provinces

3 Command
HQ: Stanleyville
Area: Orientale Province
Kivu Province

2 Command
HQ: Leopoldville
Area: Leopoldville Province
Equateur Province

Aviation Militaire de la FP (Avimil)
HQ: N'Dolo Airport, Leopoldville

Garrison Troops
Infantry Battalions
Reconnaissance Squadrons
Heavy Mortar Platoons
Transport Company
Signals Company
Military Police Company
Logistics Unit

Garrison Troops
Infantry Battalions
Reconnaissance Squadrons
Heavy Mortar Platoons
Transport Company
Signals Company
Military Police Company
Logistics Unit

Garrison Troops
Infantry Battalions
Reconnaissance Squadrons
Heavy Mortar Platoons
Transport Company
Signals Company
Military Police Company
Logistics Unit

Independent Brigade
HQ: Thysville

Gendarmerie
Gendarme Battalions

Gendarmerie
Gendarme Battalions

Gendarmerie
Gendarme Battalions

FP Strength at Independence
1,100 Belgian Officers / NCOs
Garrison Troops: 13,000
Gendarmerie: 10,000

were approximately 13,000 garrison and 10,000 gendarme troops by 1960. The garrison troops in each command area generally consisted of a number of infantry battalions equipped with Belgian FN Mauser rifles, supported by reconnaissance squadrons equipped with armoured cars, heavy mortar platoons equipped with 4.2-inch mortars, combat engineer companies, transport companies and military police companies. The troops were accommodated in military bases within the larger towns and the headquarters of the command itself. The gendarme force in each command area consisted of a battalion of the former territorial service troops, with its headquarters located at the Command Headquarters (HQ). Gendarme companies, platoons and sections were deployed throughout the districts and territories within the two provinces allocated to the command. 1 Command, with forces levied or recruited mainly from members of the Baluba and Lulua tribes, was headquartered at Elisabethville and was responsible for Katanga and Kasai provinces; 2 Command, with forces levied or recruited mainly from members of the Bakongo and Bambala tribes, was headquartered at Leopoldville and was responsible for Leopoldville and Equateur provinces; and 3 Command, with forces levied or recruited mainly from the Bakusu tribe, was headquartered at Stanleyville with an area of responsibility covering Orientale and Kivu provinces. The Independent Brigade, consisting of the training unit troops at Camp Hardy in Thysville was also capable of providing manpower as required.

During 1940 the FP recognized the need for air support for the force and an aviation wing known as the *Aviation Militaire de la Force Publique* (Avi or Avimil) was established at N'Dolo airport in Leopoldville. Avimil's role included the transportation of passengers, medical supplies and other goods, as well as liaison flights and reconnaissance missions for the FP. By independence Avimil had eleven light liaison aircraft available, including De

practice of recruiting new members from outside the Congo ceased as well. As a result recruits served in tribally mixed units with no more than a quarter of each company coming from the province in which their unit served. This, together with the military culture of strict discipline applied by expatriate Belgian officers and NCOs and the very stern application of the law of the land in their operations, contributed in no small measure to the discipline and relative calm that prevailed within the ranks of the FP at independence.

In the late 1950s the FP was reorganized and three territorial *groupements*, groups or commands, were established. Each command was responsible for two provinces and had operational control over both the garrison and the gendarme troops within its area. An additional force, known as the Independent Brigade and stationed at the training base in Thysville, Leopoldville province, provided the FP with the capacity to deploy additional troops to areas of the country where they were most needed. In total there

An FP platoon on parade, Stanleyville, 1950s. *Source*: J.P. Sonck collection

Officer Commanding 5 Battalion with his NCOs, Camp Charles, Stanleyville, 1950s. *Source*: J.P. Sonck collection

Kamina base, 1960, with Fouga Magister, C-119 Boxcar and DC-3 Dakota. *Source*: Daniel Brackx collection (www.belgian-wings.be)

Havilland Doves, three Sikorsky S-55/H-19 helicopters, three Alouette II helicopters, as well as two Piper Super Cubs on loan from the Belgian Army. At independence on 30 June 1960, the command of Avimil was transferred to the new government of the Republic of the Congo, and it continued to fulfil this role until 20 July 1960 when non-Congolese personnel and operational aircraft were ordered by the senior Belgian air force officer in the Congo to assemble at the Belgian sovereign air base at Kamina. These aircraft were then transferred to Elisabethville, and turned over to the newly independent state of Katanga.

Lieutenant-General Émile Janssens, a Belgian officer, commanded the FP as independence approached and his leadership cadre consisted of mostly Belgian officers and senior NCOs. A number of Congolese FP members had, however, been promoted to the ranks of warrant officer and senior NCO and approximately 20 Congolese candidate officers were at military schools in Belgium. In the absence of any agreement to the contrary between the various political parties in the months leading up to independence, it was evident that both the Belgian government and the Congolese political parties had accepted that the existing state of affairs in the FP would continue for some time after independence.

The Belgian Armed Forces (BAF)

The harsh lessons of the invasion and occupation of Belgium during the Second World War had made collective security a priority for Belgian foreign policy and, as a safeguard against Belgium being invaded again, two large military bases at Kamina and Kitona were established in the Belgian Congo from 1954. Viewed as a national redoubt, these bases were intended to enable the survival and rebuilding of military forces if Belgium was ever invaded again.

Belgian Air Force Sycamore helicopter at Kamina base, late 1950s.
Source: Daniel Brackx collection (www.belgian-wings.be)

Paracommandos parading in Leopoldville, 1959.
Source: Michal Neyt collection

Officers of 1 Para Battalion at Kamina, June 1960.
Source: Michal Neyt collection

Entrance to Kitona base during ONUC deployment.
Source: www.unmultimedia.org

Kamina base, situated in Katanga, covered an area of 300 square kilometres and was divided into an air force sector, an army sector, a central zone and a hydroelectric plant at Kilubi. In addition to its strategic location in Africa on the southern flank of NATO and its capacity to survive a nuclear attack, Kamina base was also regarded as an ideal location for the training of Belgian air force pilots. The flying school provided initial and advanced flight training as well as basic weaponry training; to this end it was equipped with 55 T-6 Harvard aircraft with a later addition of 18 French-built Fouga Magister jet trainers. The Belgian air force also deployed transport aircraft, mostly Dakota DC-3s and Fairchild C-119 Flying Boxcars, to the Congo for paratroop training and logistical support missions. In addition, the Belgian air force ran a weekly transport service with a DC-4 Skymaster from Brussels to Kamina via Tripoli, Cairo and Leopoldville. The Army Sector housed a fully equipped army facility through which battalion-size paratroop and paracommando units rotated on an annual basis. The Belgian military base at Kitona, located in the Congo river estuary, also rotated paratroop and paracommando units, safeguarded the deepwater port of Matadi and secured the maritime lifeline into the interior of the country.

The presence of individuals and units of the Belgian air force, the Belgian army and the Belgian navy in the Belgian Congo became an accepted norm within the country from the 1950s. While individual Belgian officers and NCOs were also seconded to FP units, others served in staff posts in the various headquarters and base areas. By independence, therefore, the BAF were familiar with the terrain and conditions within the country.

Regarding the future of the Belgian armed forces in the Congo after independence, Resolution 13 of the round table conference between the Belgian government and Congolese political parties, held in Brussels in January–February 1960 made provision for a general treaty of friendship, assistance and co-operation to be concluded between the Congo and Belgium as well as the provision of a Belgium technical mission to the Congo to co-ordinate all technical (including military) and economic assistance. The treaty was signed on 29 June 1960 and within its framework of special conventions, an agreement was reached that both Kamina and Kitona bases would remain sovereign Belgian military bases after independence.

CHAPTER THREE:
THE ROAD TO INDEPENDENCE

Political Parties Evolve

The post-Second World War wave of nationalism and the impetus for self-rule and independence that had swept across the African continent seemed to have bypassed the Congo until 1955, when a publication by a Belgian academic sparked a sequence of political events that ultimately led to the Congo's independence five years later. Professor van Bilsen of the University Institute for Overseas Territories in Antwerp published a book entitled *Un Plan de Trente Ans pour l'Emancipation Politique de l'Afrique Belge* (A Thirty-Year Plan for the Political Emancipation of Belgian Africa) in which he criticized the Belgian government for the lack of any plan for the colony's future. Included in his critique was the accusation that it was the Belgian government's fault that there were no Congolese doctors, veterinarians, engineers, functionaries and, significantly, military officers. He argued that, under the prevailing circumstances, it would take at least 30 years to prepare the Belgian Congo for independence, as he was of the opinion that the elite in the country were at least a generation behind their counterparts in the British and French territories in Africa. He proposed a federal political system of government that included the Belgian-mandated countries of Rwanda and Burundi as he felt that the country was too large for a centralized government and the two mandated territories were not economically viable on their own. He was also of the opinion that the existing colonial administration of the Congo practised many of the elements of a federal system in any event.

While the Belgian response to this publication was ambivalent at best, its publication triggered a process within the Congo wherein Congolese tribal and political groups began to publish and propagate their political, social and economic ideals. The first manifesto, published in a newspaper know as the *Conscience Africaine*, was the product of a Bangala association and it espoused an end to discrimination, a Congolese state representing Congolese aspirations, democracy and equality, as well as sincere co-operation between Belgium and the Congo. The second, the so-called Counter Manifesto, a product of Joseph Kasavubu and ABAKO (*Alliance de Bakongo*), a separatist, federalist political party based on the Bakongo tribe, was more strident and demanded *émancipation*, political rights and participation in government within a federal system, and a commonwealth approach to future relations with Belgium. The two manifestos engendered wide initial interest but their value lay perhaps more in the fact that they created a political awareness rather than achieving any concrete political gains.

The political process in the Congo advanced when a 1957 decree enabled the governor-general to establish local community councils and as a result municipal elections took place in the major towns and cities. Cultural organizations and associations

Patrice Lumumba, Congo's first prime minister, 1960. *Source*: API

A convoy of Belgian refugees takes a break while escaping to Northern Rhodesia. *Source*: API

A Sabena Boeing 707 aircraft used in the evacuation of the 34,000 refugees. *Source*: Daniel Brackx collection (www.belgian-wings.be)

based largely on tribal affiliations transcended into political organizations.

The Political Divide

The essence of the political divide, and the subsequent conflict in the Congo, now revolved around two poles: the Pan-Africanist approach in which a unitary, centralized state was emphasized on the one hand, and a federalist, separatist view which largely coincided with the tribal nationalism, on the other. The main political parties that emerged over this period included the MNC (*Mouvement National Congolais*), a party in favour of a strong central government for a future Congo, established in 1958 and led by Patrice Lumumba from the Stanleyville region. Separatist, federalist parties including ABAKO, representing the Bakongo of the southwestern Congo, established in 1956 and led by Joseph Kasavubu; Moise Tshombe's CONAKAT

Belgian refugees airlifted to Salisbury, Rhodesia by Royal Rhodesian Air Force DC-3 Dakota. *Source*: RRAF archives

ANC soldiers, carrying Belgian-made Mauser rifles, parade in Coquilhatville, capital of Equator province. *Source*: API

(*Confédération des Associations du Katanga*) party which had its political base among the Lunda tribe in southern Katanga; the BALUBAKAT (*Association des Balubas du Katanga*) based on the Baluba tribe in northern Katanga and led by Jason Sendwe; and the MNC-Kalonji (*Mouvement National Congolaise-Kalonji*), a separatist, federalist political party based on the Baluba in South Kasai province and led by Albert Kalonji. An additional eight political parties, representing unions of political movements, with federalist and moderate political aims, including political parties with European membership, also emerged during this time. The Elisabethville community council elections, contested between a Bangala tribal association and ABAKO, were won by the latter and Joseph Kasavubu became the mayor of Dendale in Leopoldville. He used his inaugural speech in April 1958 to highlight a number of perceived political discrepancies on the national Congolese political level, including the absence of Congolese officers in the military, and to make hitherto unheard of demands for a general election.

The Belgian response to this challenge was to convene a study group whose mandate it was to examine the political situation in the Congo and make conclusions that would guide the Belgian government's subsequent action. The commission made its recommendations known in February 1959, a trifle late, as the political momentum towards independence had taken on a life of its own by then, fuelled by three events. The first was the attendance by many Congolese at the International Exposition in Brussels where they were able to mix freely with Belgians, observe them and compare them to Congolese and exchange political views. The second event was a speech by General de Gaulle, the French prime minister, in Congo Brazzaville, wherein he spoke candidly with the French Congolese about political independence and was reputed to have stated that anyone who wished to achieve independence should be granted this wish. Two days later, a grouping of Belgian Congolese political parties submitted a motion to the Belgian minister for the Congo demanding social, economic and political reforms, representation on the Belgian study group and a timetable with dates for the decolonization of

the Congo. They also rejected any notion of a federal Congo and expressed their strong preference for a single unitary state. The third event was the Pan-African Conference held in Accra, Ghana in December 1958 to which representatives of ABAKO and MNC were invited. Kasavubu, the ABAKO representative, could not make the conference but Patrice Lumumba, the MNC leader, attended and was received and treated as a dignitary. During his speech at the conference he stated that the aim of the MNC was to "liberate" the Congolese people from Belgium and to achieve independence.

On his return to the Congo Lumumba made an inflammatory speech in Leopoldville, emphasizing that the Congolese people should take the political initiative into their own hands. The speech, given at a time of dire economic circumstance and unemployment within the urban population of Leopoldville, enflamed the simmering discontent brought about by the economic decline of the colony. In January 1959 the first riots took place in Leopoldville after an ABAKO political meeting had been banned. Upon hearing this, the crowd took to the streets and people and property were attacked indiscriminately over a period of two days. Europeans in Leopoldville, who were also targeted, armed and organized themselves and stood guard over vital locations throughout the city before calm was restored. Up to 49 people were killed and in excess of 200 were wounded during the rampage. The report of the Belgian parliamentary commission of inquiry into the riots cited the immediate and underlying social and political causes of the unrest, and recommended certain reorganization in the police force, proposed alternative means of intervention on the part of the military in possible future events of this nature, and a range of political and social measures that could be instituted to prevent a repeat of such incidents. The second outcome of the riots was that the leaders of ABAKO were arrested and flown to Belgium, effectively leading to the temporary dissolution of the party. They were, however, released later without a trial. A third outcome was a declaration on 13 January 1959, by both the king of Belgium and the government of Belgium, committing themselves to lead the Congolese to independence. The new government

Armoured cars parade through Leopoldville during a parade aimed at showing critics that the ANC was a well-disciplined force. *Source*: API

structure leading to independence was formulated and the future Congo government, consisting of local, territorial and provincial councils and a chamber of deputies and a senate on national level was described. Elections for local councils and the senate were scheduled to take place during 1959.

Conflict and Violence

While political developments were progressing apace between the Belgian government and the major political parties, inter-tribal conflict and violence aimed at Belgians in the Congo began to affect the political process. In Kasai province, tensions between the Baluba and Bena Lulua tribes in the capital Luluabourg escalated due to the ascendancy of the Baluba over the Bena Lulua in administrative and business positions. This jealousy and anger culminated in the arrest, in August 1959, of Albert Kalonji the president of the MNC-Kasai. Shortly thereafter rioting broke out in Luluabourg and the tension, which can be traced to an age-old conflict between the two tribes, spread to other major centres, including Tshikapa, Bakwanga, Albertville, Jadotville, Elisabethville and Leopoldville, where Baluba and Bena Lulua co-existed. While this situation cannot be directly or necessarily ascribed to the political process itself, the tensions which abounded within the Congo at the time certainly facilitated the outbreak of this conflict, which continued unabated as independence approached.

In October 1959 the MNC held its congress in Stanleyville. Lumumba's fiery oratory fanned inflamed emotions and anti-Belgian sentiment among the attendees. In the resulting riots property was extensively damaged, 26 people were killed and over 100 Congolese and Belgians were wounded. On 1 November 1959 Lumumba was arrested for inciting the riot but the unrest seemed to have achieved its own momentum and violence continued in one form or another throughout the pre-independence period with Belgians bearing the brunt of this politically inspired uprising.

The December 1959 elections on city and territory level took place throughout the Congo and were characterized by a distinct lack of violence and bloodshed. The results indicated that local circumstances where the voting took place played a major role in the election outcomes. In Elisabethville, where ABAKO boycotted the election, only 31% of the electorate voted; while in Katanga as a whole 82% of the registered voters cast their ballots. In addition, approximately 70% of the electorate voted for local candidates who were not affiliated to national political parties, a clear indication of the predominance of local leadership over national cohesion.

Belgians in the Congo

Very little has been recorded or published about the position of the approximately 125,000 Europeans, particularly Belgians in the Congo, at this point of the political process. The Belgian settlers

UN-sponsored talks between Cyrille Adoula, prime minister of the Republic of the Congo (second from left) and Moise Tshombe, president of Katanga (second from right), Kitona.
Source: www.unmultimedia.org

Robert Gardiner, Officer-in-Charge, UN Operation in the Congo (ONUC), addressing a memorial parade for Dag Hammarskjöld. Seated (right to left) are: Colonel Joseph Mobutu, Prime Minister Cyrille Adoula, President Joseph Kasavubu (Republic of the Congo); and Lieutenant-General Kebbede Guebre (of Ethiopia), ONUC force commander.
Source: www.unmultimedia.org

Four armed Leopoldville policemen batter a demonstrator, during anti-American demonstrations, November 1962.
Source: API

into action, took up arms together with his labourers and became the commander of one of the indigenous mercenary units which conducted military operations over the next seven years, culminating in what was later referred to as the mercenary rebellion in 1967. Other settlers, uncertain over the future stability of the Congo and hampered by the restrictive decree that only allowed residents to transfer the equivalent of US$200 per month to their families in Belgium, terminated their Congolese careers and moved back to Belgium in significant numbers. Over the months preceding independence on 30 June 1960 Sabena, the Belgian national carrier, was forced to charter aircraft in order to move these large numbers of returning settlers back to Belgium. Essential skills that were required to bolster the new government were being lost as a result of the political uncertainty and violence.

in the Congo, who occupied the skilled and semi-skilled positions on every level throughout the civil service and the private sector, had intended mostly to remain after independence. This intent was evident despite the fact that they had been required to pay large deposits to the Belgian government in order to work in the Congo, had effectively relinquished any political rights they had in Belgium or the Congo, were not permitted to own private property in the Congo and had not received the benefit of a representative voice at the conferences and meetings arranged between the Congolese political parties and the Belgian government on the future of the country. A feeling of isolation and anger set in among those settlers who regarded the Congo as their permanent home. One such settler, Jean Schramme, a planter from the Maniema district in eastern Congo who had lived in the Congo for most of his life felt these perceived injustices, translated them

Independence

The next step on the road to independence was the round table conference held in Brussels in January and February 1960, which was attended by 55 Belgian and 96 Congolese delegates. Only 12 of the Congolese delegates had any education beyond high-school level and their average age was 35 years. Despite the major differences between personalities and policies, agreements were reached and 16 resolutions were passed, the most pressing of which were Resolution 1 and Resolution 2 which set 30 June 1960 as the date on which the Congo would become independent. The first Congolese government on national level would consist of a chamber of deputies and a senate, and would be formed in accordance with the results of the provincial elections to be held

ONUC sentry at Elisabethville airport gate.
Source: www.unmultimedia.org

ONUC sentry on duty at the Albertville airport.
Source: www.unmultimedia.org

Irish troops (ONUC) guarding the *Banque du Congo* in Kolwezi.
Source: www.unmultimedia.org

in May 1960. Resolution 13 guaranteed the future of the Belgian sovereign bases at Kamina and Kitona, while Resolution 15 provided for the future status of Belgian administrative officials in the Congo and determined that they should fall under the authority of the Congolese government. The general response to the outcome of the Round Table Conference was enthusiasm on the part of the Congolese and incredulity on the part of the Belgian population in the country. Notwithstanding the content of the resolutions, the effect thereof amounted to a continuance of non-political control over the Congo by Belgium at the cost of relinquishing political control.

Public confidence in the political process was reduced when it was learned that the Belgian government, as a precaution, had strengthened the paracommando, paratroop, army and aviation forces in the two Belgian bases in May 1960. While from a military perspective such a deployment made absolute sense, particularly in view of the volatile atmosphere in the country, it was also evident that Congolese politicians elected to draw whatever inferences from this deployment that they could in order to bolster their own political goals. Political capital was made out of inflammatory oratory, posturing and confrontational rhetoric which targeted the Belgian colonial power, leading to the establishment and reinforcement of the perception among the restive populace that the source of all the inequities, challenges and hardships visited upon them in the past were to be ascribed to the Belgian government, the missionaries and the European settlers. Strident demands were made on the Belgian government by ABAKO, and the MNC called for the departure of the Belgian military reinforcements in the Congo, stating that General Émile Janssens, the commander of the FP, and his troops were capable of fulfilling the tasks required of them without any Belgian reinforcements. To all intents and purposes, therefore, all the political parties at this point accepted that the *status quo* regarding the FP at least would continue after independence.

Despite the all-encompassing uncertainty that beset the Congo during this period, voting in the first national election took place during May 1960. The MNC-Lumumba won 38 seats in the chamber of deputies which, together with its allied parties adding another 26 seats, enabled the party to control the Orientale, Kivu and Kasai provinces and register an accepted majority of 64 seats in the chamber, despite the fact that 69 of the 137 seats were required for a majority. During June 1960 political manoeuvring and jostling took place as the political parties edged towards accommodations and confrontations aimed at strengthening their personal and party political positions in the new government. By 23 June the MNC-Lumumba and allied parties had succeeded in garnering sufficient support for the Belgian government to call on Patrice Lumumba to form the new Congolese government. The resulting coalition government consisted of 24 ministers and 10 secretaries of state with Lumumba appointed as the prime minister and minister of defence, and Joseph Kasavubu, the ABAKO leader, elected as the first president of the country. On 30 June the Belgian Congo became the Democratic Republic of the Congo and a day later Patrice Lumumba cabled the United Nations (UN), requesting membership, to which the organization responded unanimously and positively six days later.

The Congolese body politic at independence had very little political maturity and no political infrastructure or tradition to speak of. In addition, there was no real feeling of Congolese nationalism and very little in the way of national cohesion. The future of the Congo, as the country with the highest standard of living in Africa at independence, was indeed dependent on the maintenance of a delicate balance between the Belgians in the skilled positions and the Congolese as the providers of unskilled labour. No cadre of Congolese administrators, professionals, teachers and similar vocations on which the development of a state is dependent existed and it was assumed that the Belgians would provide this capacity in the foreseeable future. Thus, while political independence had been achieved, this was of little value until administrative, social and economic independence followed.

CHAPTER FOUR:
MILITARY AND POLITICAL AFTERMATH OF INDEPENDENCE

The FP Mutiny

Within days of independence the FP, bulwark of stability in the Congo, had mutinied and violence had spread throughout the country, resulting in extensive damage to life, limb and property. This in turn affected the ability of the administration to deliver on the more mundane responsibilities required of any government: administrative efficiency, social harmony and upliftment, judicial supremacy and economic stability.

Weighed down under the responsibility of having to maintain law and order among the population of the Congo, the FP were stretched to the limit in the lead-up to the independence celebrations. In addition, there was no evidence to indicate that their existing conditions of service, the staffing of the leadership cadre by Belgians or the living circumstances applicable to the FP before independence would change. The soldiers had also undoubtedly learned of the promotion, with benefits, of their counterparts in other government departments from lowly clerical posts to executive appointments almost overnight, as the new government sought to fill the staffing vacuum left by the departed Belgians. Finally, the FP had been required to participate in a large number of military parades and ceremonial activities during the independence festivities while other civil servants had reaped the benefits of the four-day public holiday over this period.

The pressure brought about by this situation proved too much for the FP. On 5 July 1960 the first uprising within the ranks of the soldiers occurred as soldiers at Camp Leopold II in Leopoldville and at Camp Hardy in Thysville refused to obey their Belgian officers, demanded the resignation of General Janssens, the dismissal of Belgian officers who had been appointed to advise the cabinet, and the replacement of every white FP officer and NCO by Congolese officers. The FP mutineers seized weapons, left their barracks and occupied the telephone exchange, the radio station and N'Djili airport in Leopoldville. News of the mutiny also spread swiftly over the FP radio net and similar uprisings took place in the military bases in Stanleyville, at Kongolo in Katanga, at Camp General Gilliard in Luluabourg, as well as in Goma. Crowds of local civilians followed the FP example and also began to rampage through urban centres.

The occupation of N'Djili airport in Leopoldville and the roadblocks set up by marauding soldiers effectively blocked off any perceived avenue of escape for those wishing to exit the country by air from the capital. As an alternative, boat rides across the Congo river to Congo Brazzaville were attempted but these were also blocked by renegade soldiers. These actions in turn led

The first UN leadership cadre, ready for departure at Amman airport, Jordan. *Source*: www.unmultimedia.org

Soldiers of the Gurkha Regiment, Indian Brigade disembarking in the Congo as part of the ONUC forces.
Source: Unknown Danish ONUC soldier, Alf Blume collection

Ralf Bunche, UN special representative in the Congo and General Carl von Horn, commander of UN Forces in Congo.
Source: www.unmultimedia.org

Colonel Mobutu, ANC chief of staff, announcing on 14 September 1960 that he is assuming power until 31 December 1960.
Source: API

Malayan Ferret armoured cars arriving in the Congo.
Source: Unknown Danish ONUC soldier, Alf Blume collection

to the first wave of mass panic and an exodus of the European and non-Congolese African population commenced. Mutineers and crowds of locals regarded anyone who looked to be of European descent as a legitimate target on which to vent their emotions and many refugees were injured. Public services throughout the country, including transportation, mail and communications were seriously disrupted and food supplies were threatened. The consuming desire of the remaining Belgians was to get their wives and children out of the Congo and many civil servants who had intended to stay after independence changed their minds overnight and left.

In an effort to end the mutiny and appease the rioters, Patrice Lumumba removed the 1,000-odd European officers and NCOs from the command structure of the FP and fired them—although a few remained as advisers—and replaced them with Congolese NCOs. On 8 July former FP sergeant-major Victor Lundula, a Lumumba supporter, was promoted to the rank of general and appointed commander-in-chief of the newly designated *Armée Nationale Congolaise* (ANC). Joseph Mobutu, a former sergeant in

the FP, was promoted to the rank of colonel and appointed chief of staff. The fact that the newly promoted ANC officer cadre didn't have the military skills to bring any soldier accused of contravening the military code to court in effect speaks volumes as to the gaping vacuum that had been left after the Belgian officers and NCOs had been fired. Officership, leadership and the tactics, and indeed strategic insights required of incumbents in such positions, are the product of years of training and practical application. Such skills and experiences are not gained overnight. These new officers were appointed mainly on the basis of their seniority as NCOs and a number were elected. The demands were, therefore, met by Lumumba with promises of salary increases and promotion but, more importantly, the prime minister also deflected criticism and laid the blame for the uprising on the Belgian officers and other external enemies.

Within two weeks of independence, the new army had degenerated, in many cases, into armed gangs of renegades whose loyalties were to local strongmen, ethnic groups, or regions, rather than to the national government. The mutiny acted as a catalyst to the simmering unrest created as a result of unfulfilled expectations among the wider population and this can be regarded as the harbinger of the chain of tragic events that beset the Congo thereafter. The unrest in the Congo revealed the deep division, anxieties, jealousy and animosity between the various tribes and, devoid of any recognizable element with which law and order could be applied and enforced (as they were used to in the pre-independence days), the citizenry of the various areas within the Congo exploited the vacuum in order to benefit themselves financially and otherwise.

The Belgian Military Response

Viewed from the perspective of the Belgian government and its armed forces, the actions unfolding in the Congo after independence were detrimental to their national, economic and strategic interests and would obviously not have been viewed in a favourable light by the Belgian electorate. As a consequence, decisive action was required and indeed forthcoming as Belgian military operations were initiated. The initial military tasks undertaken included actions to stabilize the country, to receive and evacuate Belgian citizens and to protect military and economic assets within the Congo. Once the numbers of evacuees had decreased to the extent that air transport aircraft became available, Belgian military operations included the disarmament of ANC soldiers and the reintroduction of former FP officers and NCOs into ANC units.

In addition to the Belgian forces already deployed in the Congo, approximately 1,800 additional soldiers from reserve units were mobilized on 9 July 1960, including the independent paracommando companies and 5 Paracommando Battalion, and airlifted to the Congo. Belgian air force and army units from the neighbouring UN trustee territory of Rwanda and Burundi were also moved into the Congo to help safeguard lives and establish security perimeters in Congolese cities. The C-47 and C-119 military transport aircraft already in the Congo were used to transfer refugees to the main centres in the country and to effect internal troop movements.

From 10 July until the end of the month Belgian paracommando and paratroop units and sub-units conducted seven parachute assault operations, in which soldiers parachuted onto various objectives; three assault-landing operations, in which military transport aircraft were employed to assault an objective by short-landing the aircraft; and six airlift operations in which soldiers disembarked from commercial or military aircraft after landing on an airfield. Parachute assault operations, involving a total of 825 jumpers, were carried out in Luluabourg, where several hundred Europeans who had been besieged in the main hotel were rescued; at Kabalo in northern Katanga where a group of Europeans held hostage in a train were freed; and in Kikwit, Manono, Kindu and Bunia, to rescue civilians and disarm the ANC. Most drops were preceded by Harvard aircraft strafing the drop zone with machine-gun fire to suppress enemy fire in preparation for the combat jumps.

An assault-landing operation was conducted in conjunction with a road operation in Leopoldville on 13 July to retake N'Djili airport and secure it in order to safeguard the evacuation of refugees from the country. In Coquilhatville and Boende, European citizens were rescued and FP units disarmed during assault-landing operations. Airlift operations aimed at rescuing civilian hostages and disarming FP units took place throughout the country between 10 July and the end of the month, as did a number of road operations. A railway patrol from Luluabourg to Port Francqui and back on 15 July was also undertaken. Belgian paratroopers and commandos, acting in response to an appeal from Premier Moise Tshombe of Katanga province, also attacked mutinous Congolese soldiers in Elisabethville after six Europeans had been killed.

Operation Mangrove

The Belgian seaborne operation in the Matadi port over this period is significant, more for its unintended consequences than for its tactical success. The port itself and the rail link to Leopoldville had been effectively closed by a rail strike. Mutinying FP units in the area, on the lookout for any armed Belgians against whom reprisal could be meted out, were conducting violent searches. Within days, however, the majority of the Europeans in Matadi and vicinity had been evacuated via merchant vessels and any remaining Europeans were in all probability there by choice. From a military search-and-rescue perspective therefore, any military operation with this aim was not required. The strategic significance of the 'loss' of the country's Atlantic port as well as its rail and river links into the interior obviously weighed heavily on the military planners, so on 10 July 1960 Operation Mangrove was launched. The objective was to retake Matadi port, disarm FP mutineers and ensure the security of the rail and river links to Leopoldville. A joint force consisting of three Belgian navy Algerine-type minesweepers, each armed with a 102mm gun

ONUC troops with a 40mm Bofors anti-aircraft gun. Belgian and ANC forces used such weapons against each other during Operation Mangrove. *Source*: Unknown Danish ONUC soldier, Alf Blume collection

An armed Belgian Harvard, similar to those that took part in Operation Mangrove. *Source*: Daniel Brackx collection (www.belgian-wings.be)

and two 40mm Bofors anti-aircraft guns, together with two barges carrying an infantry company of the Ardennes Chasseur Regiment and a company of Prince Leopold's 12th Line Regiment, and supported by Harvard aircraft from Kitona base attacked Matadi. At the same time a force of 6 Commando Battalion based at Kitona attacked the port at Boma. The targets selected for the operation included Camp Redjaf, the FP/ANC base located above the port itself and manned by 357 men with access to eight 40mm Bofors anti-aircraft artillery pieces, 16 20mm Oerlikon guns and 75mm recoilless guns.

The assault force went ashore without the benefit of tactical surprise and heavy fighting ensued. Resistance was significant and the return fire from anti-aircraft guns deployed by the FP/ANC on the high ground around the port damaged one of the minesweepers. The FP radio network was effective and the FP/ANC commander at Camp Redjaf succeeded in mobilizing a reserve force from Camp Hardy at Thysville which was only stopped by air attacks from the Harvard aircraft. The port of Matadi was extensively damaged during the operation and the country's gas supplies were engulfed in flames.

By nightfall the Belgian forces re-embarked and withdrew to Boma without having achieved their objective. The outcome of

Swedish air force ONUC members offloading a J-29 at Kamina base. *Source*: www.unmultimedia.org

odd abandoned at Kamina base) and one C-124 aircraft with 34 passengers on board. The actual number of Belgian, ANC and civilian casualties and losses over this period is not known.

The United Nations Involvement

While the Belgian government was concerned about the safety of its citizens inside the Congo and the protection of its economic interests, the Congolese government perceived the Belgian military operations as an illegal invasion of a sovereign country. The new prime minister became convinced that Belgium was trying to reassert its colonial control over the country. President Kasavubu and Prime Minister Lumumba demanded the withdrawal of the Belgian troops and, when this was not carried out promptly, requested military assistance from the United States. This was cautiously refused with President Dwight Eisenhower recommending that the UN should be approached for assistance.

A Congolese government cable was forwarded to the UN on 12 July 1960 soliciting urgent UN military assistance. The UN responded by passing a Security Council resolution on 14 July giving Secretary-General Dag Hammarskjöld a mandate to restore law and order in the Congo. This provided the mandate for the establishment of *Organisation des Nations Unies au Congo* (ONUC), the UN force charged with providing military and technical assistance to the armed forces of the Democratic Republic of Congo. On 22 July a second resolution called on Belgium to withdraw its troops from the Congo.

By 30 July approximately 10,000 UN troops had been ferried into the Congo by 132 USAF C-130 and C-119 and nine Soviet Ilyushin Il-18 flights. The military airlift of ONUC forces into the Congo was primarily undertaken by the USAF and within a month 14,500 troops from Ethiopia, Ghana, Guinea, Ireland, Liberia, Mali, Morocco, Sudan, Sweden, and Tunisia had been deployed. At its peak the force consisted of troops from more than 30 countries, with India, Indonesia, Malaysia, Nigeria and the United Arab Republic among the major contributors. Ralph Bunche, a career diplomat, was nominated as the first UN special representative of the secretary-general in the Congo and General Carl von Horn, a Swedish officer serving with UN forces in the Middle East, was appointed the ONUC military commander.

In the absence of any formal military directive General von Horn formulated his task as follows: ONUC troops were to rapidly replace the Belgian troops in the Congo; thereafter they

this operation was significant in that both the FP and the civilian radio networks broadcast the FP success, inciting their listeners to seek retribution against any Belgians in their areas. The result was that many Europeans located in the north of the country, in towns such as Boende and Ikela along the Tshuapa river, were beaten and raped as they gathered at airfields in anticipation of being rescued. The situation was only resolved when Colonel Mobutu, the ANC chief of staff personally intervened to quell the unrest, thus enabling the refugees to be peacefully evacuated.

The Evacuation

The evacuation of Belgians from N'Djili airport in Leopoldville to Brussels required the assistance of Sabena. Despite the imposition of flight, landing and refuelling restrictions by African states sympathetic towards the government of Congo. Sabena's entire long-haul fleet of five Boeing-707 aircraft was committed to the emergency flights to and from the Congo after 9 July. Sabena and the Belgian air force evacuated 34,484 civilians—a quarter of all the Europeans in the Congo—over the next month while the Royal Rhodesian air force evacuated approximately 2,000 refugees from Northern Rhodesia to Salisbury and Bulawayo.

By the end of August the Belgian air force had flown 3,075 hours on 860 missions and had moved 3,735 troops and 460 tons of supplies. A number of Harvard aircraft were flown to Bujumbura, Rwanda; Belgian troops were returned to Belgium via this route as well. The bulk of the Belgian troops at Kamina, however, returned to Belgium via Sabena and the Belgian air force while others were lifted directly to Brussels with the assistance of USAF C-130s and C-124s. On 29 August 1960 Major-General Gheysen, the commander of Belgian troops in the Congo, withdrew from Kamina to Bujumbura. The rescue operation was over at a cost of one helicopter, three Harvard aircraft (with a further 20-

would take the place of the unreliable ANC forces, curb their undesirable activities and train them to become a reliable force; thirdly ONUC forces were to establish their own freedom of movement throughout the country; and lastly the force was to be in a position to prevent any unilateral interference from outside the country, an indirect reference to the possible intervention of the Soviet Union. In reality, the ambiguities of the mandate, the political limitations imposed on the military, the size of the country, poor communications and a lack of an effective central authority in the country, all left the ONUC force commanders without the wherewithal to actually fulfil the military mission as envisaged by General von Horn.

UN Tunisian troops unload food aid for victims of the conflict between the Luluas and Balubas in Kasai province, Luluabourg, Kasai. *Source*: www.unmultimedia.org

A Security Council resolution, on 9 August, called on Belgium to carry out an immediate troop withdrawal and added that ONUC would not seek to influence the outcome of any internal conflict. By implication, this meant that ONUC would not intervene in the matter of the Katangan secession. The outcome was that the Belgian troops vacated the Congo by the end of August, to be replaced by ONUC troops, and the Belgian contingent at Kamina base was withdrawn. The independence of the Congo had cost Belgium both its sovereign bases in Africa. The only force that remained consisted of 600 Belgian troops.

The Secessions—Katanga and South Kasai

The FP mutiny, the Belgian military operations inside the country and the exodus of skilled Belgians would in all probability have been a robust challenge for any newly independent state in Africa in the 1960s. Unfortunately the new government became preoccupied with obtaining external assistance to quell the 'Belgian threat', so the increasingly serious administrative problems and inter-tribal animosity were largely ignored until the country was rent politically asunder and large numbers of citizens were in danger of starving due to economic paralysis.

On 11 July 1960 the province of Katanga formally proclaimed its independence from the Congo. This extended and ferocious military conflict (which is discussed in the next chapter) almost bankrupted the UN. A second secession was precipitated nine days later by the inability of the central government to restore law and order at the diamond mines in Bakwanga, in the Kasai province, where Albert Kalonji, the MNC-Kalonji leader had unsuccessfully

appealed to Lumumba to send assistance. Members of the Bena Lulua tribe had rampaged among members of his Baluba tribe, indiscriminately killing men, women and children. Enraged at the inability of the central government to protect his subjects, Kalonji declared his independence from the central government and the Kingdom of South Kasai—the world's second largest producer of gem diamonds and its largest producer of industrial diamonds—was born.

In an effort to neutralize this, Lumumba ordered ANC units to advance on Kasai from Stanleyville, Leopoldville and Luluabourg to end the secession by force. After arriving in Bakwanga in late August, ANC troops and their leaders also went on the rampage, killing Baluba men, women and children, looting and burning the countryside to compensate for their non-existent logistic support. Lumumba's greatest affront and, arguably, his gravest political error was his decision to accept an offer of eleven Ilyushin Il-14 aircraft and a promise of 100 cargo vehicles from the Soviet Union, and then to fly over 200 more loyal ANC troops from his support base in Stanleyville to Bakwanga, via Luluabourg, to bolster ANC forces rampaging through the Baluba villages. This action brought about two consequences: a condemnation, described by the secretary-general of the UN as genocide on the one hand, and a more active interest in the country by the Cold War rivals on the other.

The first hastily deployed UN forces did manage to achieve a shaky truce between the two belligerents, and the more than 120,000 displaced refugees did receive medical and food aid from the UN to stave off imminent famine in the area. The secession dragged on for almost two years but the UN forces managed to negate any major violence by acting as a blocking force between the warring parties. The dilemma of the professional soldiers among the UN forces in the Congo, and in South Kasai in particular, is aptly expressed by a British army major seconded to the Third Brigade of the Royal Nigerian Army deployed in Kasai province in July 1961: "The role of the UN soldiers in the Congo is one that soldiers have not had to experience before … [It] is not internal security; it is to provide moral support to the ANC … We were sent to the Congo as policemen to help the central government troops maintain law and order, only to find from bitter experience that the main and practically only threats to peace came from the [government] troops themselves."[2]

Anarchy

The anarchy that had spread through much of the country was exacerbated by the personal and political differences between Kasavubu, the president, and Lumumba, the prime minister. Particularly divisive was Lumumba's insistence on the utilization of ONUC forces to end the Katanga and Kasai secessions, despite the fact that the UN mandate did not permit it, and his decision to use loyal ANC units to launch a major offensive against both Katanga and Kasai.

As a consequence, President Kasavubu announced the dismissal of Lumumba, Vice-Prime Minister Antoine Gizenga and several others from the government on 5 September 1960. Kasavubu appointed Joseph Ileo, a former MNC stalwart and supporter of Lumumba, as prime minister and Colonel Mobutu as head of the ANC. Lumumba and his cabinet responded by accusing Kasavubu of high treason and called for a parliamentary vote to dismiss him. Parliament refused to confirm the dismissal of either Lumumba or Kasavubu, seeking instead to bring about an accommodation between the two parties. After a week's deadlock,

however, Colonel Mobutu stepped in and announced, on 14 September, that he was assuming power in the Congo until the end of the year.

Mobutu emphasized that his action was not an army coup but a peaceful revolution during which the country would be run by a group of technicians. He demanded the departure of Soviet and Eastern European diplomatic personnel within 48 hours and the release of political prisoners. The period of government by Mobutu's College of Commissioners was, however, also marked by constant political conflict. The legitimacy of the government was challenged by political factions within the Congo as well as in more radical African states and communist bloc countries. Relations between the college and the UN deteriorated and the government's inability to regain any significant amount of authority or credibility enabled the two secessionist states to strengthen their administrations and military capabilities.

The seeds of further dissent and secession in the northeast of the country were being sown as the Lumumbists in the government decided to establish themselves at Stanleyville. Antoine Gizenga, an MNC loyalist, left for Stanleyville on 13 November to form a rival national government. Soon thereafter, Lumumba, who had been under house arrest since his dismissal by Kasavubu, also left for Stanleyville but was arrested, jailed, and eventually transferred to Katanga, where he was assassinated in January 1961. His assassination, by unknown assailants, when announced on 13 February 1961, prompted anarchy in many areas of the country and elevated him internationally to the status of a Cold War martyr.

The prolonged political crisis facing the government was resolved on 9 February 1961 when the College of Commissioners was dissolved and a provisional government was formed by Joseph Ileo. The events that had led to this eventual outcome over the past six months had so weakened the central government that it was unable to exert its authority much beyond the provinces of Leopoldville and Equateur.

2   Lawson, R., *Strange Soldiering*, Hodder & Stroughton, 1963, p 31.

CHAPTER FIVE:

MILITARY OPERATIONS TO END KATANGA'S SECESSION, 1960–1963

Secession in Katanga and the Developing Military Situation

Katanga did not escape the FP mutiny or the general anarchy that followed. On 8 July 1960 elements of the FP in Kongolo in northern Katanga threatened their European officers and, two days later, Congolese civilians in Kabalo, a town south of Kongolo, tried to stop the departure of a train to Elisabethville carrying 250 Europeans. The next evening soldiers at Camp Massart in Elisabethville mutinied, resulting in the deaths of seven people, including the Italian consul. Riots also broke out at Shinkolobwe during the evening of 10 July and Europeans were ordered to

evacuate this mining town as well as Kolwezi to its north. The outlook for the large number of Europeans in the mineral-rich province was sombre; they generally were left with two options: remain or flee. Despite calls for calm in Katanga, European volunteers organized themselves as a means of self-defence, especially in Jadotville northwest of Elisabethville. Europeans in Elisabethville also gathered in groups and during the night of 9 July up to 2,000 people congregated at the Collège St François de Sales. On the other hand, the number of Europeans departing to Northern Rhodesia by any means possible also increased alarmingly.

Katangan gendarmerie volunteer recruits drill near Elisabethville, Katanga. *Source*: API

Ethiopian troops (ONUC) inside Kamina base.
Source: www.unmultimedia.org

A Katangan air force Fouga Magister flight with Moise Tshombe in the rear seat. *Source*: Daniel Brackx collection (www.belgian-wings.be)

A Katangan air force DC-3 Dakota.
Source: Daniel Brackx collection (www.belgian-wings.be)

On 10 July a reinforced company of Belgian paratroopers from 1 Paratroop Battalion, under command of Major Guy Weber, was airlifted from Kamina base into Elisabethville and through an aggressive advance into the city suppressed the mutiny and returned a measure of control. The next day, 11 July, Moise Tshombe, the province's political leader, ceded power to maintain law and order to the military under command of Major Weber. Weber now became Tshombe's military adviser while also accepting responsibility to coordinate the activities of the ANC (FP), the gendarmerie, the police and the BAF in Katanga. That same evening Tshombe proclaimed the independence of Katanga, and stated that Belgium would be of great assistance if it could re-establish order and public safety and furnish technical, financial and military support.

On 12 July 1960 Colonel Champion, the chief of the Belgian Forces in Katanga, was authorized to mobilize all Belgian citizens in Katanga between the ages of 25 and 45 in order to restore the Katangan economy. After a visit by the deputy *chef de cabinet* of the Belgian prime minister, the Belgian Technical Mission (MISTEBEL) was established on 20 July. MISTEBEL and its successor, the Technical Assistance Bureau, thus became the Belgian command post for Belgian activities in Katanga; it included a Brussels police officer to organize the Katanga *Sûreté*, a professor to advise on legal matters, Major Weber, and R. Rothchild, a Belgian diplomat. Belgians also occupied posts as advisers to Katangan ministers. While the Belgian government did not officially recognize Katanga, it was compelled by its interests and the deployment of Belgians to Katanga to act as if this was the case. Diplomatically, Belgium also convinced its allies to pressurize the UN to halt the invasion of Katanga by pro-Lumumbist ANC forces.

The Belgian military forces in Katanga now moved swiftly to regain control over the new state and by 13 July Jadotville had been reoccupied, the ANC (FP) in Kamina base had been disarmed and a paratroop descent and rescue operation had taken place in Kabalo. The citizens of Kongolo in the north of Katanga were issued an ultimatum after the town had been pillaged once the Europeans had been evacuated. Colonel Crèvecoeur, a *Force Publique* officer, was appointed as the commander of the Katangan army on 13 July. The head of the Belgian Chiefs of Staff declared that the Belgian forces present in Elisabethville were at the disposal of Tshombe to protect all persons and goods, and that refugees should return to the towns. Two days later Arthur Gilson, the Belgian defence minister, authorized Belgian military forces in Katanga to occupy all important centres, particularly Kolwezi and the rail depots of Sakania and Dilolo.

On 14 July, after an aircraft carrying President Kasavubu and Prime Minister Lumumba had been refused landing rights in Katanga, the central government of the Congo declared that they had broken off diplomatic relations with Belgium, going on to request Premier Khrushchev of the Soviet Union to maintain a close watch over developments in the Congo. Needless to say, this was not taken kindly by the Soviet Union's Cold War rival.

Two Katangese gendarmes watch as a Katangan woman strikes an Indian ONUC soldier at a roadblock Elisabethville, 1962. *Source*: API

ONUC and the Military Threat to Katanga

The military situation in Katanga in July 1960 was daunting to say the least. There was some concern that the last Belgian troops deployed to protect Belgian economic interests would be forced to withdraw as a result of the arrival of the ONUC troops. This in turn would enable the ANC to move against Katanga in force from Kivu to the north or from South Kasai, or both, under command of the central Congolese government. Belgian and Katangan efforts were understandably focused on delaying the withdrawal of Belgian troops and the deployment of ONUC troops to Katanga for as long as was possible. A simultaneous effort was also initiated to develop a military force with which to defend the territorial integrity of the new state before the withdrawal of the Belgian troops.

Colonel Crèvecoeur, a former FP officer who had been appointed to command the Katangan gendarmerie, now called on former FP officers to return to the country from Belgium to join the newly formed Katanga armed forces. Belgium also seconded almost 200 serving members of the Belgium gendarmerie and regular Belgian army officers to Katanga via MISTEBEL. These men were organized into units known as *groupes mobiles*, consisting of approximately 20 Belgians and 80 Katangans in mounted jeeps and light armoured vehicles and armed with FN MAG light machine guns or .30-inch Browning machine guns. The jeeps, manned by the Belgians, acted as the attacking force and were followed by the cargo vehicles which carried the Katangan component of the *groupe*. The combination of speed and firepower was highly effective against the Baluba rebels in the north of the country. These same mercenaries gained a cavalier reputation during their off-duty periods in Elisabethville, with the name *Les*

Affreux (the frightful ones) coined to describe their dress, which consisted of camouflaged jump smocks, short shorts, shoes and rolled-down socks, coupled with their bravado, beards, heavy consumption of alcohol and boastful stories.

Local volunteer Belgian settlers were also recruited to bolster the military manpower of the Katangan state and the recruitment of volunteers from the pro-Tshombe Lunda and Bayeke tribes increased to 1,500 members. In addition, the Katangan government decided to arm local tribal warriors, seconding military advisers to such units to bolster the area defence of the fledgling state.

All the former Avimil aircraft were moved from Kamina base to Leopoldville, providing the Katanga air force with nine de Havilland Doves and one S-55 helicopter. Two DC-3 Dakotas came from the Belgian air force. Sabena also delivered matériel to Katanga during September to top up the arms, ammunition and equipment left during August by withdrawing Belgian troops. The existing *Sûreté* radio network in Katanga was also utilized to garner and distribute military and political information.

Despite initial misgivings about ONUC, the arrival of ONUC troops in Katanga on 12 August was actually welcomed by the fledgling government, as this intervention, linked to their limited mandate, provided some measure of insulation against the ANC and, together with the ONUC ban on the use of airfields after the Kasavubu–Lumumba split occurred, prevented the ANC forces massed on Katanga's northern borders and in Stanleyville from being transported to Elisabethville in requisitioned Soviet Ilyushin aircraft.

By the end of August the Belgian troops had left the Congo and Katanga was indeed being threatened on two fronts. In the west, on the border with South Kasai, and to the north at

A DC-3 chartered by ONUC.
Source: Unknown Danish ONUC soldier, Alf Blume collection

UN Secretary-General Dag Hammarskjöld talks to his military officers in the Congo. *Source*: www.unmultimedia.org

Members of Rhodesian Civil Aviation inspect the smoking wreckage of the aircraft in which UN Secretary-General Dag Hammarskjöld died.

Kongolo, ANC forces had advanced into the anti-Tshombe areas of the breakaway state. The overland southward advance of the ANC from Stanleyville had reached the border between Kivu province and Katanga and, together with anti-Tshombe tribes in the northern parts of Katanga, had occupied the town of Kongolo. Here the offensive bogged down as a result of logistic difficulties and the spate of looting and pillaging undertaken by the ANC forces. In response, Katangan aircraft flown by European mercenaries attacked and scattered the ANC forces in Kongolo. The front became static with a temporary stalemate ensuing.

This stalemate gave rise to the development of the third threat: the armed Baluba insurrection against the Katangan government. Fuelled more by a desire to rid themselves of Lunda domination in the province than by ideology, the threat was so widespread that by December the north of Katanga was no longer under effective government control. It was acknowledged that the maintenance of law and order in Kabalo, Manono, Malemba-Nkulu, Luena

and Bakama was essentially in the hands of the ONUC forces deployed there, despite the fact that this meant ONUC forces, contrary to their mandate, were violating the sovereignty of Katanga. In the east, alongside Lake Tanganyika, the area was regarded as dangerous. Between Albertville and Baudouinville to the south, it was also only really safe along the main road that connected the two towns. The Katangan government appealed for an alternative option to counter this evolving threat and thus it was that the era of the Congo mercenary was born.

The Mercenary Counter-offensive, 1961

The intent with the recruitment and deployment of Belgian mercenaries was to enable the Belgian military units to be rotated out of the Congo in order to comply with the UN resolution in this regard. It had become evident, however, that the concept of operations employed by the Belgian members of the Katangan gendarmerie was effective and a campaign was initiated to recruit additional forces to bolster this operational approach.

The recruitment of mercenaries took on two distinct forms: the recruitment of international mercenaries and the recruitment of French and Belgian mercenaries ('*Les Affreux*'). The international mercenary contingent was recruited primarily from South Africa and Rhodesia in early March 1961 and was based at Shinkolobwe near Jadotville. Known as the International Company, it was initially commanded by a Briton, Captain Richard Browne. The 44-man-strong unit was deployed to the north of Katanga where it achieved a significant breakthrough to Manono on 30 March and thereafter succeeded in conducting successful area operations against the ANC at Nyunzi, Ntemba and Kongolo. However, the company commander, a platoon commander and 28 other ranks were captured by Ethiopian ONUC soldiers on 7 April after landing at Kabalo airfield.

In late April, the much expanded International Compmay was divided into five platoons, or commandos, under Lardant (HQ), Hoare, Wicks, Lombard and Browne, and each equipped with around seven armed jeeps and the troops issued with 7.62mm FN rifles, 9mm Uzi sub-machine guns, 3.5-inch rocket launchers and 60mm mortars. 4 Commando, comprising 120 predominantly

Irish troops mobilize for ONUC duty. *Source*: www.unmultimedia.org

F-86 Sabre jets of the Imperial Ethiopian Air Force arrive at Leopoldville for ONUC duty. The commander of the UN Force, Lieutenant-General Sean McKeown, (centre) chats with fellow officers at N'Djili airport. *Source*: www.unmultimedia.org

South African and British mercenaries, was commanded by Captain Mike Hoare, a South African resident of Irish descent who had served as a British officer in Burma during the Second World War. While operations conducted by these units were directed at headquarter level by Belgian officers, the mercenary company and its sub-units were deployed independently in offensive operations against the Baluba rebellion and the ANC in the north.

The attempt to lessen the dependence on Belgian forces began to take shape in early 1961 with the recruitment of the first French mercenaries. This led to contemplation whether the supreme command of the Katangan Gendarmerie should not be entrusted to Frenchman Colonel Roger Trinquier, a regular soldier in the French army and a revolutionary warfare specialist. This initiative was eventually thwarted by vigorous Belgian opposition but did not stop other former and serving French military and police officers, NCOs and men, veterans of the Indochina and the Algerian conflicts, from entering service in the Katangan gendarmerie and bringing their not inconsequential military and covert-action skills to bear during operations against ANC forces. Two of the most notable members of this fraternity included Major Roger Faulques and a former policeman with Algerian experience by the name of Bob Denard. A training centre was established at Shinkolobwe by the French which resulted in the influx of a large number of *Organisation de l'Ármée Secrète* (OAS) members after the abortive Algerian coup in April 1961. Bob Denard took over command of the French 'Red Devils' at the end of 1961, infusing a more direct, aggressive approach to combat than his predecessors.

A further source of manpower for the Katangan military came from the settlers who, together with young Congolese militia they had recruited and trained, mobilized as military units. Organized along similar lines to the *Force Publique*, these units had the added advantage of a local understanding of the terrain and the culture. The first such group, the 'Leopard Battalion', was established by Belgian plantation owner Jean Schramme (later promoted to lieutenant-colonel), and commenced operations against the ANC in mid 1961 along the main route between Albertville and Kapona. The unit was organized into platoons of approximately 30 Congolese led by a young European officer and an older NCO with up to 15 years' experience in the *Force Publique*. The unit conducted semi-autonomous and successful operations 'in the bush' for extended periods.

On 7 and 8 January 1961, 600 ANC troops based in Stanleyville crossed the northern Katangan border and captured Manono. By implication this meant that they had penetrated areas held by the Katangan gendarmerie and the ONUC forces without any resistance. A government of the newly constituted Luluaba province was then installed in Manono. During the rest of January attempts were made to organize the administration of the new province and prepare for the expected Katangan counter-offensive. Local youths were recruited and armed to supplement the available ANC troops but by the time the mercenary counter-offensive commenced the Luluaba government had a mere 160 soldiers at its disposal.

While Colonel Crèvecoeur, the Belgian officer in command of the Katangan gendarmerie, was in overall command of operations in Katanga, the Task Group that opened the offensive on 11

February with the capture of Mukulakulu on the main Kolwezi–Kamina route was commanded by Major Matthys, another Belgian officer. On 13 February the railway line between Lubadi and Luena was recaptured, thus enabling coal exports to start flowing again via Port Francqui. The focus of the offensive then turned.

The time taken to achieve this was in all probability due to the gradual approach followed by Katangan forces so as not to hasten any unwanted UN intervention. The ONUC force in northern Katanga, consisting of an Ethiopian battalion deployed in and around Kabalo, was outnumbered by the Katangan gendarmerie and did not, in fact, intervene. The UN commander in Katanga warned Tshombe on 27 March that the UN would oppose the use of force to take Manono. However, on 30 March Manono fell to the Katangan gendarmerie, supported by the International Company. On 2 April the first Indian contingent arrived to reinforce the ONUC position in northern Katanga. While the offensive was a success on a military level, its effect was to draw ONUC into the conflict. The subsequent capture of Captain Browne and a platoon of the International Company as well as the destruction of a barge carrying 150 Katangan gendarmes at Kabalo on 7 April is proof of this.

ONUC's Mission Changes

On 21 February 1961 the UN Security Council passed a resolution demanding the withdrawal and evacuation of all Belgian and other forces from the Congo, including mercenaries, not under UN command. In effect, this decision was directed against the existing, tenuous independence of Katanga. The government responded by mobilizing the Katangan population to counter the new threat. Whereas before, the ONUC forces had, by their passive presence, assisted in enabling the maintenance of law and order in Katanga and thereby allowing the fledgling government to act against the threats on its northern and western borders, the ONUC forces had now become a *de facto* enemy of Katanga. The ONUC presence in Katanga was strengthened with the arrival of the first troops from the Indian Brigade at Kamina base in Katanga on 2 April. This was a clear indication that ONUC intended to actively carry out the 21 February resolution. Similarly, the central government of the Congo, hitherto reasonably eager to co-exist with Katanga, signed an agreement with the UN on 17 April, effectively accepting the 21 February resolution and recognizing the necessity to reorganize the ANC with the assistance of the UN. A more hostile posture towards Katanga had evolved: to all intents and purposes, and in spite of the extremely poor relationship, it appeared that ONUC had allied with the central Congolese government against Katanga.

On the military front a period of calm and stalemate ensued while the UN forces strengthened their positions throughout Katanga. The Katangan gendarmerie was thus able to prevent any new penetrations from the north. The ONUC forces, however, succeeded in positioning themselves in such a way that they were able to 'shadow' the Katangan gendarmerie.

Operation Rumpunch

The implementation of the February 1961 Security Council resolution on the withdrawal of foreign military personnel and mercenaries in the Katangan gendarmerie was taken a step further in June1961 once Colonel Bjorn Egge, a Norwegian ONUC officer arrived in the Congo. The matter was discussed between Egge and Colonel Crèvecoeur, the head of the Katangan gendarmerie, and a plan developed which was agreed between ONUC and the majority of Katangan ministers. Foreign military personnel and mercenaries would be gradually withdrawn from the Katangan gendarmerie and replaced by officers and men, probably French-speaking Tunisians, nominated to the positions stated by ONUC. The UN resolution and the plan affected 520 of the 11,000 men in the Katangan gendarmerie. The Katangan government naturally delayed the implementation of this for as long as possible as it was in their interests to do so. It was almost inevitable that the ONUC force would ultimately be required to act on its own initiative.

An incident between ONUC forces and Katangan gendarmerie on 26 August in Elisabethville set off a sequence of events which led to a worsening of the existing cordial relationship between ONUC and the Katangan government. A group of Katangan gendarmerie, under command of two Belgian officers, was ordered to dig trenches near the runway at the Elisabethville airport. This activity was detected by the troops of ONUC's Irish Battalion deployed at the location, whereupon the gendarmes were subsequently disarmed and the officers expelled from the area. This more aggressive approach to the conduct of their mandate led the Katangan gendarmerie to deduce that an ONUC military operation was imminent. The deduction was correct as ONUC launched Operation Rumpunch in the early hours of 28 August. The primary objective of the operation was to arrest all foreign military officers and NCOs in Katanga, while the secondary objectives were to detain Godfried Munongo, the Katangan interior minister, on a temporary basis, and temporarily occupy the radio and post office in Elisabethville in order to neutralize the telephone exchange and disrupt telephone traffic.

At this point the UN Command in Katanga estimated that the Katangan gendarmerie consisted of 13,000 men deployed as follows: 3,000 in Elisabethville; 2,000 in Jadotville and Shinkolobwe; 1,000 in Kolwezi; 800 in Manono, Kongolo, Kipushi and Baudouinville, and 400 each in Kabango and Kapanga. ONUC forces had approximately 5,000 men from the Indian Brigade and the Irish, Swedish and the Ethiopian battalions deployed in Elisabethville, Albertville, Kamina base, Kabalo, Manono and Jadotville.

The Katangan forces, expecting the operation to commence on 29 August, were taken by surprise and within an hour of the 0500 H-Hour on 28 August the radio station, post office and telephone exchange had been seized and a cordon set up around Godfried Munongo's residence. Tshombe yielded to pressure and declared in a radio broadcast that all foreign military officers in the Katangan gendarmerie were to be dismissed forthwith. The

Katangan casualties of the clashes with ONUC at Elisabethville.
Source: API

A Katangan Fouga Magister, captured and vandalized by UN troops.
Source: Unknown Danish ONUC soldier, Alf Blume collection

cordon around the selected locations was lifted and Katangan officers were placed in command of the gendarmerie. Large numbers of foreign military personnel and mercenaries were detained and expelled from the country over the next days, only to return shortly thereafter. In addition, other mercenaries changed into civilian clothes and disappeared among the population or covertly continued their duties. Within a week between 250 and 338 Europeans on the list of 520 foreign military personnel and mercenaries had been expelled and the balance had disappeared, only to return a few days later to take up their former roles. The number of foreign officers and NCOs who were actually repatriated to their home countries and remained there is difficult to determine. Operation Rumpunch was therefore only partially successful; the implementation of the UN Security Council resolution was not completely fulfilled.

Pursuant to the operation the relations between Tshombe and Dr O'Brien, the UN representative in Elisabethville, deteriorated markedly, with a spate of political and diplomatic incidents between the parties. In this atmosphere of increased hostility ONUC reinforced its troops in Elisabethville by deploying an additional battalion of Gurkhas from the Indian Brigade. It was evident that it was only a matter of time before further animosity was to break out between ONUC and the Katangan gendarmerie.

Operation Marthor

The relationship between ONUC and the Katangan government deteriorated further and incidents of provocation between the two military forces as well as between Katangan residents and ONUC troops escalated until early September 1961. After one particularly tense period, ONUC planners, including Dr. O'Brian, developed the concept of operations for Operation Marthor (after the Hindi word meaning 'smash'), a military offensive to round up the remaining foreign mercenaries in Katanga, to neutralize Tshombe and to bring him and the representatives of the central government to the negotiating table in order to end the secession of Katanga. In short, the operation was aimed at terminating the Katanga secession. The plan called for the seizure of Radio Katanga, the arrest of the Katangan minister of information and

a raid on the offices of the internal security force by 1 Dogra Group (Indian Brigade) and a company of the Gurkha Regiment (GR) (Indian Brigade); the seizure of the radio transmitter, the detention of the Katangan minister of finance and the securing of the refugee camp by the Irish Battalion Group; and the seizure of the Elisabethville radio transmitter and the minister of interior by 12 Swedish Battalion Group plus one company of the GR.

The operation commenced at 0400 on 13 September in and around Elisabethville but it was soon evident that the Katangan forces were expecting the attacks and were fully prepared for them. The attack on the post office and Radio Katanga was initially successful but the Katangan forces counter-attacked, with Radio Katanga being set alight by mortar fire. The post office was kept under heavy direct fire from surrounding buildings throughout the night. ONUC aircraft were warned off by anti-aircraft fire from the city.

A day later the ONUC forces at the radio station, consisting of two officers and 24 other ranks of the Irish Battalion were forced to surrender to the Katangan gendarmerie and a Katangan air force Fouga Magister bombed the Elisabethville airport three times, destroying one Katangan DC-4, one ONUC DC-4 and damaging a third. In addition, the headquarters of ONUC's Katanga Command in Elisabethville was subjected to heavy direct fire on the night of 16 September, leading to the death of one UN soldier and six wounded. In addition the UN force commander was not able to reinforce his troops in Elisabethville: on the day the operation commenced, approximately two companies of Katangan gendarmes attacked the Irish company deployed at Jadotville to ensure the freedom of movement of ONUC forces between Elisabethville and Kolwezi. The entrenched defensive positions of the Irish company held as attacks on the troop deployment continued over the next two days. On 15 September an ONUC plan to reinforce the Jadotville garrison with two infantry companies and withdraw the troops thereafter was approved. Supplies and ammunition were replenished by helicopter and the force was dispatched on foot from Elisabethville, 141 kilometres away. The relief force was subjected to Katangan air force attacks en route and their advance was brought to a halt

ONUC troops manhandling a Willys Jeep with a mounted 106mm recoilless rifle, Elisabethville area. *Source*: www.unmultimedia.org

Operation Grand Slam. ONUC troops inspect the Bailey bridge over the Kipushi river. The permanent bridge was demolished during the withdrawal of the Katangan forces. *Source*: www.unmultimedi.org

at the bridge over the Lufira river, 15 kilometres from Jadotville, when it was discovered that it had been mined and prepared for demolition. The relief force sustained four killed, 16 wounded and four missing. The Jadotville garrison surrendered to the Belgian officers and Katangan troops on 17 September. Casualties at Jadotville included an unconfirmed number of Belgian officers and Katangans as well as 30 wounded Irish soldiers.

In northern Katanga orders were issued to the ONUC forces on 14 September to plan for the total disarmament of Katangan forces deployed in the area. On 18 September the operation to clear the gendarmerie mobile group and the police from Albertville commenced with a successful road-clearing operation to the airfield and an assault on the police camp. In Manono and Nyunzi, as at Nyemba, the Katangan gendarmerie surrendered to the ONUC forces and a total of 198 gendarmes and policemen were disarmed.

As Operation Marthor got underway in Elisabethville, the ONUC-occupied base at Kamina was also attacked by Katangan gendarmerie but the Swedish and Irish battalions deployed there succeeded in defending the base and the airport with the assistance of a company of infantry from the Indian Brigade.

Dag Hammarskjöld, the UN secretary-general, attempted to negotiate a ceasefire between ONUC forces and the Katangan gendarmerie when it became apparent that the military operation had reached stalemate. Tshombe, who had moved to Ndola in Northern Rhodesia, proposed to meet the secretary-general in Ndola in order to discuss the terms of the ceasefire. The DC-6 aircraft utilized by Hammarskjöld to fly to Ndola to meet Tshombe crashed or was shot down approximately 12 kilometres from the airport, killing 17 members of the party, including the secretary-general. Pursuant to this Mohammed Khiary, the UN Special Representative in Leopoldville, flew to Ndola on 19 September and a ceasefire agreement providing for a joint monitoring commission, the prohibition of troop movement, the exchange of prisoners and the resupply of provisions was signed between the two parties the next day. During the hostilities eleven ONUC troops and approximately 50 Katangans had been killed.

ONUC analyzed the operation and concluded that on the military level their forces did not have adequate offensive air support, artillery or armour. At times during the operation the Katangan air force, consisting of one Fouga Magister jet aircraft piloted by a mercenary, had inflicted enough damage and disruption to prevent the deployment of UN forces. It was also found that the Katangan forces had obtained a copy of the ONUC operations order, enabling them to prepare in advance for the expected ONUC offensive. ONUC commanders criticized the fact that the majority of their deployments were dictated by political ends rather than the dictates of tactics and that no single clear and comprehensive directive was addressed to them throughout 1961 that outlined the scope of their operations in the field. The over-centralization of tactical decision-making was also slated as was the lack of any clear concept of what the ONUC forces were actually supposed to do. Militarily the operation led to a stalemate but on a political level Tshombe emerged as the victor.

Operation Unokat

In the aftermath of the Katangan successes during Operation Marthor relations between the ONUC forces and Katangan officials and the local inhabitants worsened, while internationally an anti-UN campaign was initiated throughout Angola, Congo Brazzaville, Rhodesia and South Africa. The extent of the anti-UN feeling was such that in Elisabethville shopkeepers refused to sell goods to ONUC members. At the internal political level Premier Adoula assailed the ceasefire agreement between the Katangan government and ONUC and so, on 20 October, a force of 5,000 ANC troops invaded North Katanga. The ANC was largely successful and reached Albertville, but the offensive halted mainly due to the blocking actions of the Katangan gendarmerie, supported by air attacks carried out by de Havilland Doves from the Katangan air force armed with Hotchkiss and .50 inch Browning machine guns mounted on tripods inside the open hatches and homemade bombs manufactured in the mine workshops of *Union Minière du Haute Katanga*. By December, however, the number of incidents between Katangan forces and ONUC forces was such that open hostilities between the belligerents were a mere matter of time.

UN Secretary-General U Thant and ONUC officers. From left: Brigadier Ogundipe, commander of the Nigerian contingent; Brigadier Reginald Noronha, commander of the Indian Independent Brigade; Lieutenant-General Kebede Gebre (Ethiopia), commander-in-chief of the UN Forces in the Congo; Secretary-General U Thant; Major-General D. Prem Chand (India), GOC Katanga; Colonel N.L. Hederen, commander of the Swedish contingent; Major-General Kaldager (Norway), air commander; and Lieutenant-Colonel A.G. Palmquist, commander of the Swedish jet fighter unit.
Source: www.unmultimedi.org

ONUC reinforced its position in Katanga from four infantry battalions to seven by flying in forces and additional support elements from other parts of the Congo in C-124 and C-130 aircraft. Additionally, the ONUC forces now had four Ethiopian air force F-86 Sabre jets, six Swedish J-29 jet fighters and five Indian air force Canberra jet bombers available for operational use. The ground forces in Elisabethville were reorganized into two groups to facilitate command and control: No. 1 Brigade, consisting of two Swedish battalions and the Irish battalion, supported by the armoured car squadron and armoured personnel carriers of the Swedish and Irish contingents, was given the responsibility for the area east of the railway line between Elisabethville and Jadotville; No 2 Brigade, consisting of two battalions of the Indian Brigade, an Ethiopian battalion, supported by the Malaysian armoured car squadron and four Swedish armoured personnel carriers, was responsible for the area to the west of the same railway line. U Thant, the new UN secretary-general, instructed UN political representatives and military commanders in the Congo to take whatever action was required to ensure the freedom of movement of ONUC forces and the restoration of law and order so that UN resolutions could be fully implemented.

On 14 December an operational directive was issued to ONUC troops at Elisabethville to seal off the city from all directions as of 16 December. By 19 December all the listed objectives of ONUC, including the railway tunnel, Camp Massart and the Union Minière area, had been taken and occupied; the operation was regarded as a success. Outside Elisabethville, however, the ONUC forces had fared worse over the preceding week with casualties on both sides in excess of 220 dead, 58 Katangans captured and many more wounded. ONUC did clear Manono and approximately 12 kilometres of road southward to Mitwaba.

The outcome of the operation was twofold: Elisabethville was

now effectively isolated from the rest of the country and the outside world and the Katangan forces had lost control of northern Katanga to the Balubas and the Stanleyville ANC forces. Under pressure from US diplomats, Tshombe agreed to fly to Kitona to meet with Premier Adoula and, while a ceasefire was in place, signed an agreement which effectively acknowledged the end of the Katangan secession. Once back in Elisabethville, however, Tshombe declared that the agreement had to be ratified by his government before it came into effect. A watered-down version was finally passed by his government after a year.

In the interim, larger areas of northern Katanga, including Albertville, were handed over to the central Congolese government to the extent that they were in effective control of a belt of Katangan territory north of the east–west line at Manono. The areas where the Katangan forces still dominated were centred in the vicinity of Jadotville, Kolwezi and Kipushi.

Elsewhere in the Congo the potential secession by Antoine Gizenga in Stanleyville ended in February 1962 with his arrest and imprisonment. Similarly the Kingdom of South Kasai was dissolved two months later, with Albert Kalonji placed in protective custody. While the situation had stabilized in Elisabethville itself, with only sporadic incidents, including the stoning of Indian troops by local women, the ANC troops in northern Katanga were repeatedly attacked by Katangan forces led by mercenaries.

The U Thant Plan

The UN secretary-general, faced with an operation that was bankrupting the organization, submitted a programme of measures for the Congo, referred to as the 'Plan of National Reconciliation', to the Security Council in August 1962 for approval. The so-called U Thant Plan provided for a federal system of government, the division of revenue between Katanga and the central government on an equal basis, currency unification, the integration and unification of the entire Congolese army, exclusive representation abroad by the central government, the representation of all political parties in the central government and a general amnesty for political prisoners. The plan was approved by the Western representatives in the Security Council and was presented to the two opposing parties in the Congo at the end of August, to positive reaction. Throughout the remaining months of the year, however, a spate of incidents between Katangan gendarmerie and ONUC forces took place throughout Katanga which contributed to an increase in the level of hostility between the two sides and, together with Tshombe's political manoeuvring, set the scene for a final military confrontation at the end of the year.

With the erection of opposing roadblocks within Elisabethville, together with incidents where ONUC helicopters were fired upon and shot down, ONUC's freedom of movement in the city had been severely restricted. In addition, on 27 December, ONUC positions in Elisabethville and Jadotville were brought under heavy automatic and mortar fire from Katangan gendarmerie positions. This was followed, on 28 December, by the interception of a radio message wherein the commander of

Members attached to 38 Irish Battalion advance on Kipushi, Katanga, during Operation Grand Slam. *Source*: www.unmultimedia.org

A Katangan Harvard destroyed by ONUC aircraft at the airfield in Kolwezi. *Source*: www.unmultimedia.org

the Katangan gendarmerie requested the Katangan air force to bomb the Elisabethville airfield on the night of 28/29 December. The ONUC commander in Katanga responded by ordering the implementation of Operation Grand Slam.

Operation Grand Slam

The strategic intent of Operation Grand Slam was to terminate the secession of Katanga. The military component of the operation required the ONUC forces, as part of Phase One, to achieve freedom of movement in and around Elisabethville by securing Katangan gendarmerie positions throughout the city. Phase Two, if required by political and military developments, called for ONUC forces to advance on and take Jadotville and Kipushi respectively. An advance on Kolwezi had been envisioned but was postponed as it was uncertain whether the available bridging equipment would allow a force to cross the rivers between Jadotville and Kolwezi. An advance on Kipushi, to the southwest of Elisabethville, would allow the UN and the Congolese central government to control the main border crossing into Northern Rhodesia.

On 28 December 1962 Operation Grand Slam commenced and by the end of the day the central area of Elisabethville, known as the Gymnasium area, had been taken by a GR company. An

Indian battalion (4 Madras) attacked the Radio Colony, advanced on the gendarmerie base at Karavia and captured it by 1830 that evening after the defence had abandoned it. That same evening gendarmerie forces reinforced their positions in Kasapa, north of the city centre, and brought fire to bear on ONUC forces.

The next morning two companies of the GR, supported by a troop of armoured cars, advanced on and enveloped the gendarmerie forces at Kasapa and captured the position by midday. To the north of Kasapa, two companies of an Indian Battalion (4 Rajasthan Rifles), supported by a battery of heavy mortars and a platoon of machine guns, captured the key terrain around the rail and road crossing known as Martini Junction after heavy resistance and the eventual abandonment of the position by the gendarmerie. In addition, the Ethiopian Battalion, supported by two armoured car troops and a heavy mortar battery, advanced from the centre of the city along the main route to Kipushi and occupied the tactical high ground in the Simba Hills area. The 38 Irish Battalion, supported by a troop of armoured cars and a heavy mortar battery, passed through their lines and advanced up to the Kafubu river, five kilometres east of Kipushi, where the advance was halted as the bridge had been destroyed by the retreating Katangan gendarmerie. Overnight, an existing 40-foot Bailey military bridge was dismantled inside Elisabethville, transported to the Kipushi river and erected by ONUC engineers. ONUC troops occupied Kipushi by midday on 30 December. The road to the Northern Rhodesian border post was now secure.

On 30 December two companies of an Indian battalion (4 Rajasthan Rifles), supported by armoured cars, heavy mortars and a medium machine-gun platoon advanced from an area west of the main airfield and secured the important road junction at Kasenga to prevent any gendarmerie offensive operations against the airfield from an easterly direction. A third company of the battalion also secured the Kilobilobwe radio station, while the Ethiopian battalions secured Katuba and Muken to the south of the city. By the end of the day, all postal, telephone and telegraph offices, railway and radio stations as well as the National Bank of Katanga and all road access routes to the town were secure. The Katangan forces had withdrawn to Northern Rhodesia in the south and Kolwezi along the route to Dilolo on the Angolan border.

On 31 December, 18 Swedish Battalion occupied Kaminaville, effectively capturing the Kamina airbase and surrounding area; ONUC demanded that all Katangan aircraft should be handed over to the UN by 1 January 1963 otherwise they would be destroyed. By 31 December Tshombe had also returned to Katanga from a visit to Rhodesia and, on this same day, the UN secretary-general gave the approval for Phase Two of Operation Grand Slam to commence, despite having given Belgium and the United Kingdom an assurance that UN troops would not advance on Jadotville and Kolwezi beyond the Lufira river.

The ONUC Indian Brigade Group, minus two infantry battalions, was selected to undertake the advance on Jadotville and the force, consisting of motorized infantry and infantry on foot, together with armoured cars, heavy mortar and engineer support,

ONUC soldiers of the Indian Brigade boarding the US military sea transport service ship *General Blatchford* in Mombasa, Kenya. *Source*: www.unmultimedia.org

The End of Katanga's Secession

The number of mercenary officers in the Katangan gendarmerie had dwindled by now and, as the ONUC forces advanced towards Kolwezi, Tshombe met with his closest military advisers, including Jean Schramme who had retreated from Kansimba, south of Albertville on 6 January 1962, Bob Denard and Jerry Puren. The streets of Kolwezi had become congested with refugees and the defensive perimeter extended only 80 kilometres to the east of the town. Tshombe, together with his military staff, devised a plan to cater for the last days of the secession and the future. The advance of the ONUC forces was to be delayed by Schramme while Denard and his forces would withdraw to Teixeira de Souza in Angola via the border town of Dilolo, west of Kolwezi. All Katangan forces and equipment of any military value were to be moved into Angola

advanced as far as the Lukutwe river before they came under effective fire from the Katangan gendarmerie. By the evening of 1 January, however, they had reached the Lufira river, where the road and rail bridges as well as the bridge over the Tanga river had been destroyed by the Katangans. A bridgehead was established and over the next day, supplies, mortars and jeeps were ferried across the river to defend the locality and prepare a firm base for the continuation of the advance on Jadotville. The advance had been subjected to sustained and accurate fire as elements of the Katangan gendarmerie, led by mercenaries, carried out delaying operations along the axis of advance.

On 3 January the ONUC advance on Jadotville recommenced, led by a mobile group of jeeps armed with machine guns, two 106mm recoilless rifles and supported by a towed 4.2-inch mortar. A Sikorsky S-55 helicopter was used to ferry mortar ammunition forward to the weapon positions as the advance progressed. When the bridge over the Likasi river outside Jadotville was destroyed an alternative approach to the town was located through ground and air reconnaissance; the motorized forces reached the town via this route while the infantry used the railway bridge to cross the river on foot. Katangan gendarmerie had withdrawn from the town but European mining officials and local inhabitants met the ONUC forces and displayed no hostility. Jadotville was in the hands of ONUC forces and a Bailey bridge was constructed over the Lukutwe river to ensure a route to Elisabethville. The advance on Kolwezi was, however, delayed significantly as the Brigade Group had advanced almost beyond the extent of its logistic capability and despite the capture of the Kamatanda airfield ten kilometres north of Jadotville, was only resumed six days later. Shinkolobwe fell to ONUC on 13 January as the mercenaries, together with the Katangan gendarmerie, continued to steadily withdraw towards Kolwezi, destroying bridges behind them.

to form the nucleus of an army in exile. Schramme would follow after the fall of Kolwezi and, with the remaining approximately 4,000 gendarmes and 50 mercenaries, withdraw last to Dilolo where he would command the Katangan army in exile. The force would be housed in special camps in Angola while the remainder of the mercenaries would be disbanded. A constant stream of aircraft, trains and cargo vehicles conveyed what was left of the Katangan gendarmerie and their equipment, as well as the Katangan Treasury—estimated to be approximately £5 million and which was to sustain the Katangan army in exile—to Dilolo.

On 21 January, after crossing numerous obstacles on the road to Kolwezi, the ONUC advance reached the outskirts of the town where discussions between the two belligerents were held. An end to the ONUC military operations in Katanga was announced and the UN secretary-general confirmed that a reduced force would remain in the Congo to assist the central government in maintaining law and order. Four days later the last of the Katangan gendarmerie, together with Jean Schramme and the Leopard Battalion, crossed into Angola 300 kilometres west at Dilolo. The Katangan secession was over but the role of Jean Schramme, mercenaries and Katangan gendarmes in the Congo was not.

The extent to which the United States contributed towards the success of the ONUC effort is not widely publicized. On 9 July 1960, for example, the aircraft carrier USS *Wasp* sailed from Guantanamo Bay for the west coast of Africa to support the deployment of ONUC forces by air and by the time of her departure in early August, the carrier had supplied almost a million litres of fuel in support of the UN airlift. In September 1960 USS *Windham County*, a navy landing ship tank, and USS *Whitfield County* embarked 600 Malayan troops and their equipment, and disembarked them at Matadi, Republic of the Congo, on 31

October 1960. In January 1961 the USS *Hermitage*, a dock landing ship, was utilized to carry 550 tons of corn meal and powdered milk from Togo to the port at Matadi in support of the United Nations food-aid programme to combat starvation in the country. A month later the vessel, together with USS *Graham County*, a tank landing ship, embarked 500 Guinean troops of ONUC and returned them and their equipment to Conakry, Guinea. The extent of the USAF military airlift to the Congo is perhaps even more surprising: 2,310 missions which moved 63,884 personnel

and 37,202 tons of material from 33 different countries, covering a total distance of 40 million kilometres.

A reduced number of ONUC forces remained in the Congo until 30 June 1964, whereupon the military life of ONUC expired. At its height ONUC had deployed 20,000 troops and while its mandate was to provide military and administrative services, the organization had been sucked into a confused and violent civil war, leading to the death of a secretary-general and 234 ONUC personnel.

CHAPTER SIX:
MILITARY OPERATIONS TO END THE REBELLION IN KIVU AND ORIENTALE PROVINCES, 1964

The Short-lived Peace

The end of the Katanga secession did not bring peace to the Congo. President Joseph Kasavubu and Lumumba's successor, Prime Minister Cyrille Adoula, needed to install an inclusive national government that reconciled the numerous and varied interests within the Congo. In addition, an effective military force was required with which the country's sovereignty and law and order could be guaranteed while the political process took its course. These goals proved to be elusive though and a wave of rebellions broke out in various parts of the country by the time

the last ONUC forces had left the country in June 1964. An uprising in Kikwit in the Kwilu area of the Leopoldville province, led by Pierre Mulele, is said to have been the first large-scale peasant insurrection in an independent African state. Espousing a combination of Marxism and Maoism heavily imbued with magic-religious overtones, the Kwilu revolt or Mulele rebellion, although limited in extent, continued until December 1965, and the threat to the central government did not end until Mulele's execution in October 1968. Secondly, the force of 4,000 Katangan gendarmes which had relocated to Teixeira de Souza in northeastern Angola at

A Congolese rebel army leader is hauled off by ANC soldiers during a round-up in Kindu, November 1964. *Source*: API

Colonel Vandewalle, commander of 5 Mechanized Brigade.
Source: Brassinne collection

Colonel Liegeois, commander of Lima 1.
Source: Brassinne collection

Colonel Lamouline (left), commander of Lima 2.
Source: Brassinne collection

the end of the Katangan secession was also poised as a latent threat to the government. In addition, the attempts by the government to quell disputes within the eastern provinces of the country had given rise to the advent of the National Liberation Committee (NLC) in Stanleyville, led by Christophe Gbenye and Gaston Soumialot, both members of the Lumumbist MNC party.

By 1963 the ANC, as the national army, had achieved some semblance of unity under the command of Major-General Mobutu but the 30,000 men were largely ineffectual on the battlefield due to poor training and equally poor leadership. Better known for their cruelty towards unarmed civilians, the ANC was not equal to the multiple threats that were developing throughout the country.

To help deal with the insurgencies, former Katangan secessionist leader Moise Tshombe, living in exile in Spain, was recalled to office and arrived in the Congo on 26 June 1964, four days before the last ONUC troops left the country and within a very short period of time he was appointed prime minister of the Congo.

In an effort to assist in containing the rebellion and position aircraft in the area as a precaution against any Soviet interference, the Central Intelligence Agency (CIA) established a mercenary air force in the Congo serviced initially and operated latterly under the auspices of a Lichtenstein-incorporated company known as *Anstalt Wigmo* (WIGMO). At its height the CIA controlled all the existing Congolese T-6 fighters, numerous T-28 fighters and seven B-26 Invader light attack bombers, all piloted by mercenary pilots, the majority of whom were Cuban.

While the interests of the US and Belgium in the Congo had appeared to be diametrically opposed during the Katangan secession, both states still shared an interest in preventing the Soviet Union from dominating the Congo, and ensuring that the minerals mined in Katanga, particularly its cobalt, continued to reach US markets.

Once the Belgian government had reduced its support of the Katangan secession in 1962 and the withdrawal of the ONUC forces was imminent in 1963, the US approached Belgium with a plan to provide bilateral military assistance to the country under the auspices of the UN. When this initiative was rejected by the UN, both the US and Belgium opened military-assistance missions in the Congo in 1963. CAMAC, the Belgian mission under Colonel Logiest, provided military advisers and training for the ANC and COMISH, the US mission under Colonel Williams, provided technical assistance to improve the ANC's logistic capability.

The Fall of Stanleyville, August 1964

In July 1964 Tshombe faced three rebellions in the Congo, of which the two in the east of the country were being fanned by the brutal reprisals meted out by the ANC. During May the ANC lost Bukavu to Bufulero tribesmen marching north from Uvira and at the same time ANC reprisals against dissidents in Albertville angered the local population to the extent that they overturned the local government and executed its president. Gaston Soumialot

Major Mike Hoare, commander of 5 Commando.
Source: Brassinne collection

5 Commando officers, from left: Mike Hoare, Alistair Wicks, Ian Gordon and John Peters. *Source*: BMA

The 4.2-inch mortar platoon in the advance.
Source: Brassinne collection

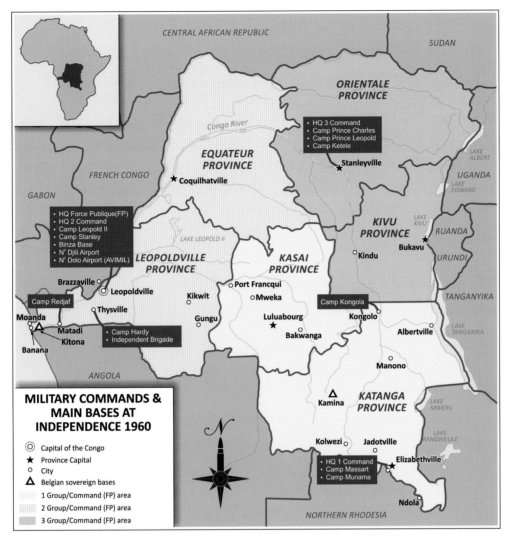

CENTRAL AFRICAN REPUBLIC

SUDAN

ORIENTALE PROVINCE

- HQ 3 Command
- Camp Prince Charles
- Camp Prince Leopold
- Camp Ketele

★ Stanleyville

LAKE ALBERT

UGANDA

LAKE EDWARD

Congo River

EQUATEUR PROVINCE

FRENCH CONGO

★ Coquilhatville

GABON

- HQ Force Publique(FP)
- HQ 2 Command
- Camp Leopold II
- Camp Stanley
- Binza Base
- N° Djili Airport
- N° Dolo Airport (AVIMIL)

LAKE LEOPOLD II

LEOPOLDVILLE PROVINCE

KASAI PROVINCE

○ Kindu

KIVU PROVINCE

LAKE KIVU

★ Bukavu

RUANDA

URUNDI

Brazzaville ○

◎ Leopoldville

Camp Redjaf

○ Thysville

Moanda ○
△
Matadi
Kitona

Banana

○ Kikwit

○ Port Francqui
○ Mweka

○ Gungu

★ Luluabourg
○ Bakwanga

Camp Kongola
Kongolo

TANGANYIKA

LAKE TANGANIKA

○ Albertville

- Camp Hardy
- Independent Brigade

○ Manono

ANGOLA

△
Kamina

KATANGA PROVINCE

LAKE MWERU

LAKE RANGWEULE

Kolwezi ○ Jadotville ○

○ Elizabethville
★

- HQ 1 Command
- Camp Massart
- Camp Munama

Ndola ○

NORTHERN RHODESIA

MILITARY COMMANDS & MAIN BASES AT INDEPENDENCE 1960

- ◎ Capital of the Congo
- ★ Province Capital
- ○ City
- △ Belgian sovereign bases
- 1 Group/Command (FP) area
- 2 Group/Command (FP) area
- 3 Group/Command (FP) area

N

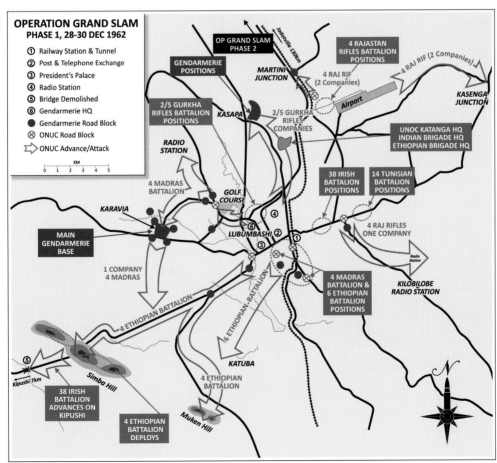

OPERATION GRAND SLAM
PHASE 1, 28-30 DEC 1962

- ① Railway Station & Tunnel
- ② Post & Telephone Exchange
- ③ President's Palace
- ④ Radio Station
- ⑤ Bridge Demolished
- ⑥ Gendarmerie HQ
- ● Gendarmerie Road Block
- ⊗ ONUC Road Block
- ⇨ ONUC Advance/Attack

KM
0 1 2 3 4 5

OP GRAND SLAM
PHASE 2

Jadotville 130km

GENDARMERIE POSITIONS

4 RAJASTAN RIFLES BATTALION POSITIONS

MARTINI JUNCTION

4 RAJ RIF (2 Companies)

4 RAJ RIF (2 Companies)

KASENGA JUNCTION

Airport

2/5 GURKHA RIFLES BATTALION POSITIONS

KASAPA

2/5 GURKHA RIFLES COMPANIES

UNOC KATANGA HQ
INDIAN BRIGADE HQ
ETHIOPIAN BRIGADE HQ

RADIO STATION

38 IRISH BATTALION POSITIONS

14 TUNISIAN BATTALION POSITIONS

4 MADRAS BATTALION

GOLF COURSE

④

KARAVIA

⑥
LUBUMBASHI ②
③

4 RAJ RIFLES ONE COMPANY

Radio Station

MAIN GENDARMERIE BASE

①

⊗

KILOBILOBE RADIO STATION

1 COMPANY 4 MADRAS

4 MADRAS BATTALION & 6 ETHIOPIAN BATTALION POSITIONS

4 ETHIOPIAN BATTALION

6 ETHIOPIAN BATTALION

⑤

Kipushi 7km

Simba Hill

38 IRISH BATTALION ADVANCES ON KIPUSHI

4 ETHIOPIAN BATTALION DEPLOYS

KATUBA

4 ETHIOPIAN BATTALION

Muken Hill

N

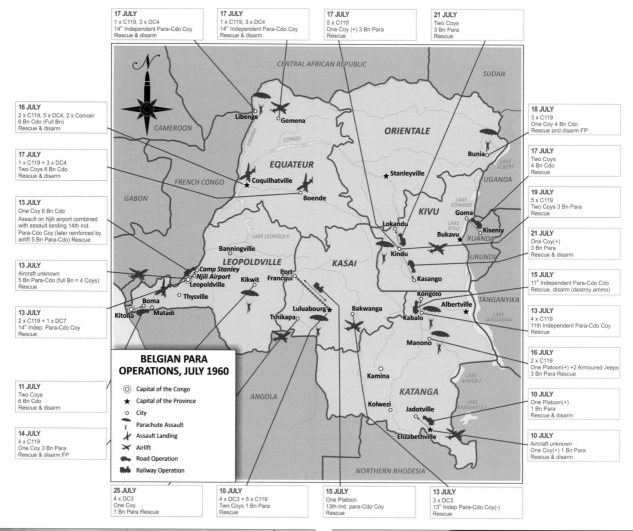

17 JULY
1 x C119, 3 x DC4
14th Independent Para-Cdo Coy
Rescue & disarm

17 JULY
1 x C119, 3 x DC4
14th Independent Para-Cdo Coy
Rescue & disarm

17 JULY
5 x C119
One Coy (+) 3 Bn Para
Rescue

21 JULY
Two Coys
3 Bn Para
Rescue

16 JULY
2 x C119, 5 x DC4, 2 x Convair
6 Bn Cdo (Full Bn)
Rescue & disarm

17 JULY
1 x C119 + 3 x DC4
Two Coys 6 Bn Cdo
Rescue & disarm

13 JULY
One Coy 6 Bn Cdo
Assault on Njili airport combined
with assault landing 14th Ind.
Para-Cdo Coy (later reinforced by
airlift 5 Bn Para-Cdo) Rescue

13 JULY
Aircraft unknown
5 Bn Para-Cdo (full Bn = 4 Coys)
Rescue

13 JULY
2 x C119 + 1 x DC7
14th Indep. Para-Cdo Coy
Rescue

11 JULY
Two Coys
6 Bn Cdo
Rescue & disarm

14 JULY
4 x C119
One Coy 3 Bn Para
Rescue & disarm FP

18 JULY
3 x C119
One Coy 4 Bn Cdo
Rescue and disarm FP

17 JULY
Two Coys
4 Bn Cdo
Rescue

19 JULY
5 x C119
Two Coys 3 Bn Para
Rescue

21 JULY
One Coy(+)
3 Bn Para
Rescue & disarm

15 JULY
11th Independent Para-Cdo Cdo
Rescue, disarm (destroy ammo)

13 JULY
4 x C119
11th Independent Para-Cdo Coy
Rescue

16 JULY
2 x C119
One Platoon(+) +2 Armoured Jeeps
3 Bn Para Rescue

10 JULY
One Platoon(+)
1 Bn Para
Rescue & disarm

10 JULY
Aircraft unknown
One Coy(+) 1 Bn Para
Rescue & disarm

BELGIAN PARA OPERATIONS, JULY 1960

◎ Capital of the Congo
★ Capital of the Province
○ City
Parachute Assault
Assault Landing
Airlift
Road Operation
Railway Operation

25 JULY
4 x DC3
One Coy
1 Bn Para Rescue

10 JULY
4 x DC3 + 5 x C119
Two Coys 1 Bn Para
Rescue

15 JULY
One Platoon
13th Ind. para-Cdo Coy
Rescue

13 JULY
3 x DC3
13th Indep Para-Cdo Coy(-)
Rescue

ONUC Scania Vabis armoured cars belonging to the Swedish contingent, Elizabethville. *Source*: Unknown Danish ONUC soldier, Alf Blume collection

A USAF C-130 transport aircraft at Kamina base. USAF aircraft ferried ONUC troops into the Congo. *Source*: Unknown Danish ONUC soldier, Alf Blume collection

Katangan homemade tank.
Source: Unknown Danish ONUC soldier, Alf Blume collection

Katangan Air Force Fouga Magister. One of these aircraft neutralized the ONUC forces in Elizabethville during Operation Marthor. *Source*: Daniel Brackx collection (www.belgian-wings.be)

The following sequence of four maps is adapted from: Odom, T.P., *Dragon Operations ...* , Levenworth Papers 14, 1988.

Indian Air Force (ONUC) Canberra bomber.
Source: Unknown Danish ONUC soldier, Alf Blume collection

Swedish Air Force (ONUC) Saab J-29.
Source: Unknown Danish ONUC soldier, Alf Blume collection

The following sequence of four maps is adapted from: Odom, T.P., *Dragon Operations ...*, Levenworth Papers 14, 1988.

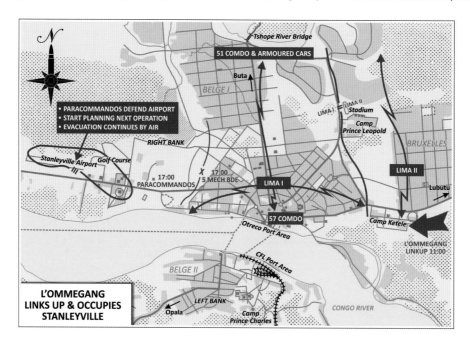

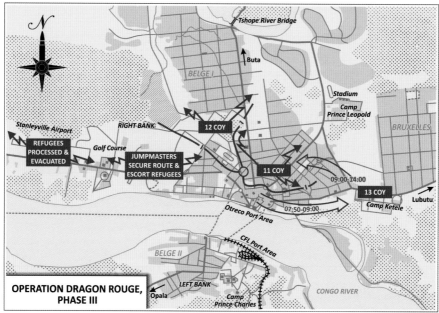

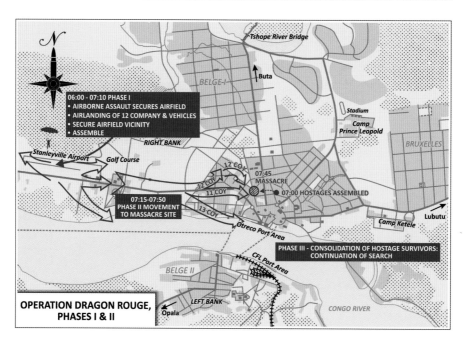

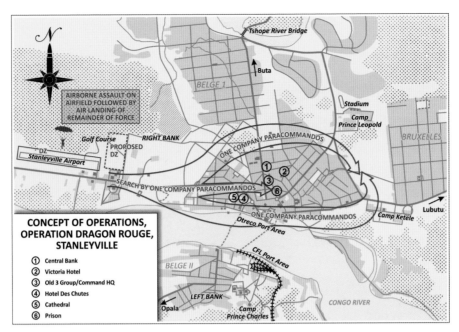

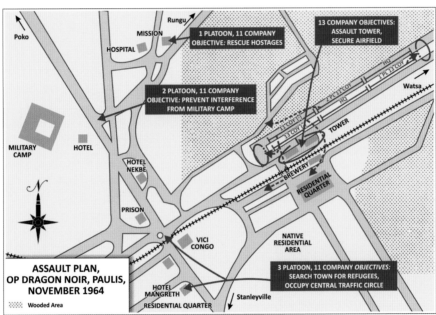

Adapted from: Odom, T.P., *Dragon Operations ...* , Levenworth Papers 14, 1988.

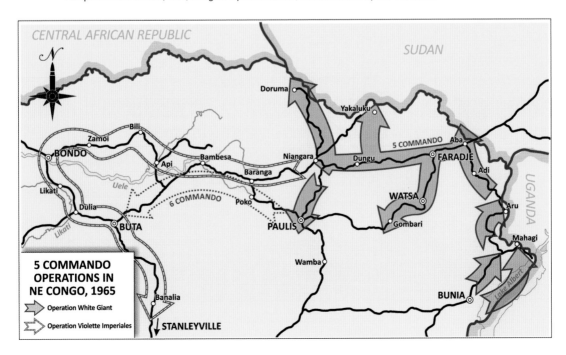

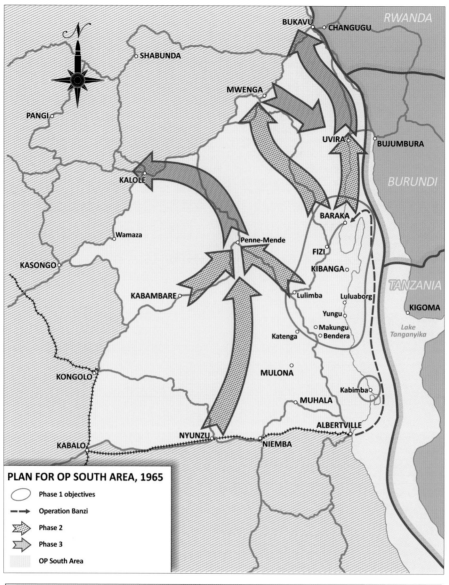

PLAN FOR OP SOUTH AREA, 1965

- Phase 1 objectives
- Operation Banzi
- Phase 2
- Phase 3
- OP South Area

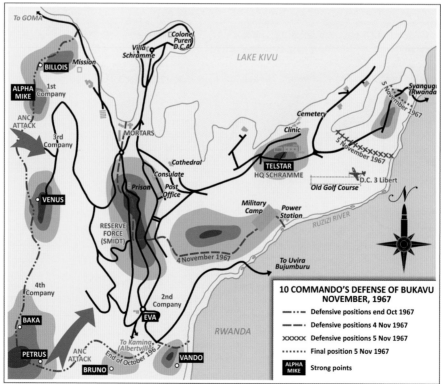

10 COMMANDO'S DEFENSE OF BUKAVU
NOVEMBER, 1967

- Defensive positions end Oct 1967
- Defensive positions 4 Nov 1967
- XXXXX Defensive positions 5 Nov 1967
- Final position 5 Nov 1967
- ALPHA MIKE Strong points

Adapted from: Honorin, M., *La Fin des Mercenaires*, Robert Laffont, Paris 1968.

Re-opening the Congo river to traffic between Bumba and Stanleyville.
Source: Michal Neyt collection

Cuban Swift Boat on Lake Tanganyika.
Source: Iain Peddle

An improvised mortar pit aboard a barge between Bumba and Stanleyville.

Above: Convoy under command of Captain Hugh van Oppen, 5 Commando, in Operation South area.
Source: Martin van Oppen collection

Left: A team of mercenaries on a 5 Commando jeep.
Source: Martin van Oppen collection

Re-opening the Congo river to traffic between Bumba and Stanleyville.
Source: Michal Neyt collection

Assortment of badges of 5 Commando, 6 Commando, 9 Commando and 10 Commando.
Source: Michal Neyt collection

A 5 Commando Ferret on the invasion barge, Operation Banzi.

Above: Colonel Roger Hardenne (maroon beret), Chief-of-Staff Operation South, inspects a WIGMO B-26. *Source*: Michal Neyt collection

Left: 5 Commando officers Captain Hugh van Oppen, Dick Hammond and Jimmy James share a joke while Bob Houcke, the French CIA pilot, looks on. Operation South area. *Source*: Martin van Oppen collection

H-21 helicopter supporting the advance. *Source*: Brassinne collection

The advance between Kindu and Lubutu. *Source*: Brassinne collection

had relocated to Bujumbura in Burundi and was quick to link the dissident activities to the National Liberation Committee (NLC) and visited Albertville to organize the rebellion. Rebel activities in the eastern provinces of Kivu and Orientale were conducted on such a scale that Baudouinville and Albertville fell to the rebels.

The NLC rebels under the leadership of Nicholas Olenga set off on a march along two routes into the interior of the Congo and the movement attracted followers, including disaffected youths, or *jeunesse*, armed with machetes and clubs. The rebels advanced on and took Kasongo before entering Kindu by the end of July 1964. The ANC forces had dispersed due in no small measure to

the powerful aura of invincibility that had been attributed to the rebels. Part of this power was derived from the dispensation, to the rebel troops, of *dawa*, or magic, by local fetishists. Followers then graduated to become Simbas, the Swahili word for lion. Armed with its perceived invulnerability against all in its path, the force of over a 1,000 Simbas under the newly promoted General Olenga, began an advance on Stanleyville.

Stanleyville, a city of 300,000 inhabitants, had a garrison of 1,500 ANC troops stationed on both banks of the Congo river, under the command of Colonel Leonard Mulamba, an outstanding and competent military leader, who was absent on duty in Bukavu. The subsequent Simba attack on Stanleyville by a small force of lightly armed *jeunesse* rattled the ANC defenders and they fled, leaving the city to the rebels. The Simba rebellion had advanced over 1,000 kilometres in a month—from Albertville to Stanleyville—and the lightly armed collection of disaffected citizens, convinced of their invincibility had succeeded in routing the country's armed forces and taking over the capital city of Orientale province. While initially the Simba rebellion appeared to have targeted Congolese rather than the approximately 1,600 Europeans in the city, this all changed on 5 August when they decided to attack the US Consulate, forcing consular staff, including the consul and the CIA representative, to seek refuge in the consulate's communications vault. The fall of Stanleyville on 5 August also meant that the river transport links between Stanleyville and the outside world, through which the main flow of commodities and export material was conveyed, had been severed. Barge traffic came to a standstill at the town of Bumba on the river, downstream from Stanleyville, and ore exports from the mines in Katanga and the port on the left bank of the river at Stanleyville were effectively terminated.

The fall of Stanleyville stunned the Congolese as well as the US and Belgian representatives in the country and galvanized them into action to assess their strategic interests in the country and the safety concerns of their citizens. It also forced the US to overcome its prejudice against Tshombe and resulted in the development of a joint US–Belgian strategy for the Congo which allowed both countries to pursue their interests and influence events at arm's length through the use of proxies.

The two powers would intervene through a mercenary-led organization to stabilize the military situation in the country. Belgium would provide logistic advisers to the special organization and train ANC units and the US would provide logistical support and enhance the means with which it could be distributed throughout the country. In addition, the crisis was to be internationalized by engaging African states and other disinterested European states.

The US established and deployed Joint Task Force LEO (JTF LEO) to the Congo on 11 August. JTF LEO, with its headquarters in Leopoldville, was commanded by Colonel Robert Teller, US Marine Corps, and consisted of a small joint staff, a protection platoon of US airborne soldiers, support elements, two H-34 helicopters and four Hercules C-130 transport aircraft. The US

Casualty evacuation. *Source*: Brassinne collection

military had, together with the CIA air force, committed a sizeable force to the conflict in the Congo.

On 14 August any reluctance on the part of the US to distance itself from the fighting was eradicated when Nicholas Olenga attacked Bukavu with a force of approximately 1,000 rebels. The rebel force advanced into the city in trucks but was repulsed by the ANC, under the command of Colonel Mulamba. Reinforced by a battalion of Katangan gendarmes airlifted into the area by JTF LEO and with the added advantage of close air support provided by CIA's T-28 aircraft, the attack failed. What was more telling, however, was the fact that during the fighting three Americans, two of whom were senior military officers, had been cut off from the city by the rebel advance and narrowly escaped being captured. The defeated Olenga blamed his defeat on the US and sent word to Stanleyville ordering the arrest and trial of all Americans in the city. The risk that any offensive against the rebels in the eastern provinces would lead to the death of the European hostages in Stanleyville and other centres outside the area of influence of the Congolese military forces had become more probable, so US military planners started entertaining alternatives to resolve the problem at hand.

The Force Development of 5 Mechanized Brigade

The development of a plan and the preparation of a force with which the Congo could regain the sovereignty of her two eastern provinces began in earnest towards the end of August 1964 with the promulgation of two directives to two vastly different role-players in the conflict. One directive, signed personally by Prime Minister Tshombe and Major-General Mobutu, the commander of the ANC, established an area of military operations within the Congo where military operations were to be conducted to restore law and order. The same missive appointed Colonel Vandewalle, the former head of the intelligence service in the Belgian Congo and a former Belgian attaché to Katanga, as military adviser to the prime minister and commander of ground and air operations in the new operational area. The subsequent delineation of the Congo into four territorial command areas plus the operational area required by the directive, made provision for military operations to be conducted in an area extending throughout well over half the country east of a general line between Port Francqui and Banzyville in the north, and north of a general line between Port Francqui–Kamina and Lake Mweru in the south. The second directive was a hand-written document signed by Major-General

4.2-inch mortar in action. *Source*: Brassinne collection

Mobutu in the presence of the prime minister and provided, on request, to Major Mike Hoare, former mercenary commander of 4 Commando in Katanga, to immediately provide 200 mercenaries with which to retake Manono, Albertville, Fizi and Baraka on Lake Tanganyika, to provide an additional 300 mercenaries to form mobile ground forces and to retake Stanleyville as part of a joint mercenary–ANC offensive. The battlefield for the offensive to retake the east was delineated and 5 Mechanized Brigade, under command of Colonel Vandewalle, was established.

The tactical headquarters of 5 Mechanized Brigade was temporarily located at Kamina base and the first, undated, operational order, issued early in September 1964, outlined the headquarters organization of the brigade and ordered the development of two sets of three combat-ready infantry battalions by 15 October and 15 November respectively. The mission of the brigade was given as the reconquest of the rebel provinces by Christmas. The force was to seize Kivu with three battalions by 30 October and Stanleyville with six battalions two months later.

The development of the forces required for the operation saw the recruitment of mercenaries in South Africa and Rhodesia, their arrival at Kamina and their training in preparation for the operation. Mike Hoare, the commander of 4 Commando during

the Katangan secession, designated his battalion of no more than 200 men as 5 Commando and sub-divided it into an eventual eight sub-units (51 through to 58 Commando), with two officers and three sergeants per commando. The serious requirement for immediate action against the rebels forced 5 Commando to deploy an untrained, unacclimatized and under-strength force, together with the support of the ANC, to retake Albertville as required by Mobutu in his directive. It was stated that there were up to 120 Belgians at risk in the town. Operation Watch-Chain, launched by Mike Hoare on 24 August with 30 men, was not a resounding success for 5 Commando. He failed to reach his target, lost two men and returned to Kamina with seven wounded soldiers. The lessons learned during the offensive were brought to the attention of the additional recruits who were arriving to make up the full strength of 5 Commando. The ANC did eventually take the city on 30 August and saved the lives of 135 Europeans. The relationship between 5 Commando and the Belgian members of the brigade was, however, not always smooth. Contrary to Hoare's agreement with Mobutu, Vandewalle chose to interpret the writ in his directive narrowly and penny-packeted the sub-units of 5 Commando throughout the geographical area of his command to form the attack or strike component of each attacking force.

The force requirements of the offensive could not be totally fulfilled by the southern African mercenary contingent and the recruitment of Belgian military and former military officers and NCOs was undertaken. The men were allocated to the leadership cadre of 5 Mechanized Brigade to be utilized in their specialized fields, including combat engineering, mortars, signals and logistics. A drive to recruit a force of mostly French, Italian, Dutch, German and Greek mercenaries was also undertaken with some success and 6 Commando, a unit that was to gain notoriety, or fame, in 1965 under the command of a returned Bob Denard, was born.

Another force which made a re-appearance from the Teixeira de Souza area of Angola was the Leopard Battalion of Jean Schramme and the additional Katangan gendarme forces that had been deployed there since the termination of the Katangan secession. Designated 10 Commando, Schramme's unit of approximately 750 Katangans was given the task of pacification operations in Kivu province.

By 14 October the organization of 5 Mechanized Brigade consisted of a brigade headquarters and staff manned by Belgian officers, as well as 5 Commando (the southern African mercenary unit with seven platoons identified from 51 to 57 Commando) commanded by Major Mike Hoare; 6 Commando (the European mercenary unit with six platoons, 61 to 65 and a platoon made up of paratroopers) commanded by Lieutenant Topor; 7 Commando of Lima 1 (consisting of a logistics team, three infantry companies levied from the Kongolo area, an armoured car squadron and an engineering squadron) under command of Lieutenant-Colonel Liegois, a Belgian officer; 8 Commando of Lima 2 (consisting of a logistics team and three infantry companies levied from the Kamina area) under command of Lieutenant-Colonel Lamouline, a Belgian officer; 9 Commando or Force Papa (consisting of a logistics team, an infantry company levied from the Manono area and an under-strength ANC infantry battalion) commanded by Major Protin, a Belgian officer; 10 Commando (the Leopard Battalion that had returned from Angola) under command of Major Schramme; and support units including a military police company, an administration company including drivers

and signallers under command of Lieutenant Lizet, a training contingent under command of Major Welo, a logistics element and a base defence element under Lieutenant Georlette. The brigade also had a combat engineering company, a company of 4.2-inch mortars and an under-strength regiment of Katangan gendarmes under its operational control.

The plan for the first phase of the offensive called for 5 Mechanized Brigade to advance from the base area of Kamina north along the Lualaba river, a tributary of the Congo, take Kindu by the end of October and then occupy the area around the town in order to deny it to the rebels. At the same time, three ANC task forces, referred to as Op Nord, Op Tshuapa and Op Kivu respectively, were required to regain control over the Eastern province by advancing from Lisala to Bumba, from Ingende to Ikele and from Bukavu towards Bunia respectively. Lastly, a force known as Op Protin would deploy to the east of the main effort to provide technical and logistical support, protect the flank of the main force from any enemy interference from the east and attack the rebel pocket at Kabambare and in the Fizi mountains. 10 Commando was to act as the brigade reserve during this phase in the vicinity of Kongolo, while defending the town and, at the same time, preparing to be operational with effect from 1 November. The plan provided for units of the Katangan Baka Regiment—11,

River crossing. *Source*: Brassinne collection

Link-up between the L'Ommegang and Dragon forces at camp Ketele, Stanleyville. *Source*: Brassinne collection

C-130 aircraft staging before Dragon Rouge jump. *Source*: BMA

Paracommando AS 24 tricycle at Stanleyville. *Source*: BMA

12, 13, 14 and 15 Commando battalions—to occupy the areas that the main force would regain in Kindu, Punia and Kibombo. Air support in the form of reconnaissance, close air support and transport was to be provided by the combined capabilities of Task Force LEO, CIA, and the Congolese tactical air force.

The main force, made up of Lima 1 and Lima 2, hastened to complete the required logistic build-up in time and move from Kamina via road, rail and air to the assembly area at Kongolo. While this was underway the command element was also required to contend with personality clashes and differences of opinion between the array of commanders from vastly different backgrounds. Notable at this point was Major Mike Hoare's disappointment that his 5 Commando was to be divided up among the various task forces to be used as the vanguard, leaving him with his headquarters, with the armoured cars and three sub-units as the vanguard of the main force. Another notable difficulty was the difference of opinion between Major Protin and Jean Schramme which caused unnecessary delays. In all, 5 Mechanized Brigade consisted of 66 Belgian army officers and NCOs and 350 mercenaries in addition to the Congolese and Katangan forces.

The Advance on Stanleyville

Notwithstanding these and the difficulties of the terrain, the river crossings and the heavy reliance on air transport, Lima 1 and 5 Commando, consisting of a motley collection of approximately 200 vehicles, crossed the start line in Kongolo on 1 November 1964 with 55, 56 and 57 Commandos as the vanguard, together with the Belgian armoured car element consisting of two Ferret and three Swedish Scania Vabis armoured cars, the latter being referred to as 'Sons of Bitches' by the English-speaking troops. The non-standard nature of the vehicles gave Colonel Vandewalle, the commander of 5 Mechanized Brigade, occasion to remark that he was of the opinion that he was actually in command of the Ommegang, a colourful annual Belgian pageant celebrated since 1549. This name has stuck in the annals of the operation.

The advance proceeded north along the western bank of the Lualaba river and reached Kindu by 5 November. The use of armoured vehicles and the firepower of the 5 Commando mercenaries, in the vanguard of the main advance, followed by a company of ANC troops in the centre and the logistic echelon thereafter, proved very successful and enabled the main force to move the 400 kilometres from Kongolo to Kindu in just seven days.

The use of the .50-inch Browning machine guns in the CIA T-28 aircraft that flew missions over Kindu effectively disrupted the rebel forces, enabled the hostages in the town to hide from the rebels and at the same time allowed the L'Ommegang forces to manoeuvre into the town under fire to engage the rebels and save hostages. The effect of close air support on the continued success of the L'Ommegang operation was cemented at Kindu. The advance was hastened substantially as a result of the discovery of dead hostages in Kibombo, a town 120 kilometres south of Kindu, and the final assault took the form of a night advance on the town. Once the town had been secured an air bridge was established in

A Paracommando guards hostage bodies in the centre of Stanleyville. *Source*: BMA

'58 Commando'. Cubans leaving Stanleyville after the search for US consulate staff. The civilian standing is a missionary. *Source*: BMA

which USAF and FATAC transport aircraft were used to airlift the Lima 2 troops as well as vehicles, ammunition and supplies as part of the logistic build-up to enable Phase Two, the 850-kilometre advance on Stanleyville, to take place from a firm base. The vital crossing over the Elila river, 20 kilometres north of the town on the main advance route to Stanleyville, was manned by 5 Commando in order to keep the route to the north open.

In the north of the country the Op Nord force, strengthened by a vanguard provided by 51 Commando, under command of Lieutenant Wilson, didn't wait for the rebels to advance on Gemena, but pushed towards Lisala to engage them. In September the mercenary-led vanguard attacked Lisala, with a company of ANC infantry in support and routed the rebels, leaving 160 dead. One mercenary was slightly wounded during the attack. After a period of patrols in and around Lisala, enabling the civilian administration to return, the Op Nord forces requested and obtained authority to advance on Bumba, reaching the town on 16 October.

The Op Tshuapa force, strengthened initially by 52 Commando under the command of Captain Siegfried Mueller, a holder of the German Iron Cross, advanced with two companies of ANC soldiers along the route from Coquilhatville to their rebel-held objective at Ikela. After an unsuccessful attack on Boende, the mercenary force withdrew to Bikili, 20 kilometres to the north, where the rebel force surrounded them. 54 Commando, whose men had seen action in Yakoma on the northern border with the Central African Republic, where they had repelled the rebels who had withdrawn with an American hostage by the name of Dr Paul Carlson, were sent south to assist 52 Commando. The combined force, together with close air support from CIA forces and under the command of Major Lemercier, a Belgian army officer, took Boende on 24 October and seized Ikela by 6 November. The force consolidated their gains and occupied defensive positions as it had been determined that they were no longer in a position to attack the left bank of Stanleyville.

In the east the Op Kivu force was reinforced by 53 Commando in late September and went into action against the attacking rebels at Kabare, 20 kilometres north of Bukavu, scattering them to the extent that they ceased to be a threat to Bukavu thereafter.

Hereafter, the road south to Uvira was cleared and the town was taken and garrisoned by the ANC and 53 Commando on 7 October. Shortly thereafter, Lieutenant-Colonel Mulamba recalled the commando to Bukavu to act as the vanguard of an advance on Lubero and Butembo, approximately 300 kilometres north of Bukavu. Butembo, with an estimated strength of 3,000 poorly armed rebels, fell to the combined force on 28 October with the loss of one mercenary and a few hundred rebels. 53 Commando spent the next few days consolidating its position in anticipation of additional tasks farther north.

The Op Protin force advanced north from Albertville and, after taking Lulimba, swung west towards Kabambare where they became stationary after a number of contacts with the rebels. Jean Schramme, with his Leopard Battalion, was tasked to advance from the Kongolo area to reinforce the effort. Advancing slowly and laying everything in its path to waste, the relief column reached its destination early in December. By this time, Protin's forces had established a firm base of local support in Kabambare itself. Operations against the rebels in this area were far from over, however, and the insurgency in this mountainous area continued.

The Plan for the Final Advance on Stanleyville

On 17 November Colonel Vandewalle was ordered to commence the approach to Stanleyville earlier than planned and capture the city on 23 November. As a result, the mercenary vanguard, together with Lima 1, Lima 2 and the remainder of the force, crossed the start line in Kindu on 19 November and proceeded at best speed north along the main road via Punia where the ferry over the Lowa river was seized and a bridgehead over the river was established. The town of Lubutu was reached on 22 November. L'Ommegang had covered the 370 kilometres in four days and had crossed rivers, weathered setbacks and swept aside all rebel ambushes and delaying positions to reach their objective. The brigade was now ordered to take Stanleyville on 23 November.

A seemingly insignificant, yet vital detail associated with the Belgian-led operation was the presence, on the ground as it were, of US military forces. While reference has already been made to the USAF air support and CIA air operations, little is ever eluded to the fact that the US army had at its disposal a certain Lieuten-

USAF C-130s participated in the evacuation from Stanleyville. *Source*: Brassinne collection

Evacuees being escorted to Stanleyville airfield. *Source*: BMA

Evacuees move on foot to the Stanleyville airfield. *Source*: BMA

ant-Colonel Rattan and his driver, who were included in the order of march of the main L'Ommegang force as observers. A second, even lesser-known fact was that in an extension to the CIA involvement in the Congo, a small ground force, consisting of 18 Cuban mercenaries and Rip Robertson, a CIA officer, joined the L'Ommegang force at Punia and accompanied the main force into Stanleyville. This force, referred to as 58 Commando by Major Mike Hoare, had been tasked to enter Stanleyville and, in an independent operation, rescue US diplomatic and other staff, including the CIA officers present in the town. In addition, approximately 150 of the vehicles, the ammunition and a large quantity of the combat rations were of US origin.

The plan for the attack on Stanleyville required the L'Ommegang force to complete the final 230-kilometre advance along the main road between Lubutu and Stanleyville during the night of 23 November in order to be in a position to attack the town as early as possible on 24 November. The orders for the final attack on Stanleyville were deliberately kept as simple as possible: Lima 1 was tasked to take the centre of the town and then advance to the airport while the armoured car platoon was to advance north to the bridge over the Tshopo river and prevent any enemy interference along the main road from the north; 5 Commando was tasked to occupy the port on the northern bank of the river and locate and man any possible crossings over the Congo river; Lima 2 was required to take Camp Ketele, the police camp and Camp Prince Leopold in order to block any advances on the centre of the town from the east; while the military police company was required to cordon off and protect the bank in the centre of the town.

The Dragon Operations

The price exacted by the rebels for the defeats along the Op Tshuapa and Op Nord routes, in particular, startled the US and Belgian political supporters of the campaign. It became all the more evident that Europeans were being executed in retribution and hostages were being taken by the rebels as they retreated eastwards. Intercepted rebel radio conversations also contained threats to kill one American for every Congolese killed. At Boende the first dead hostages were discovered and similar evidence was unearthed by the L'Ommegang force as it advanced on Kindu. Over 70 Western hostages, from as far away as Punia, had been gathered at Kindu and, as the L'Ommegang forces advanced, the rebel threats against them escalated until, on 5 November 1964, all the male hostages were taken into the street, stripped to their underwear and informed by the rebels that they were to be executed. The aggressive use of B-26 aircraft, however, panicked the rebels and they fled, leaving the hostages to find suitable hiding places until the ground advance had entered the town and rescued them.

The aggressive use of air power against rebel positions was not received kindly by the US military and political representatives in the Congo as they believed that such actions would increase the likelihood that the rebels would kill American citizens in retaliation. Task Force LEO withdrew two of its Hercules C-130 aircraft for a period of time from operations in an effort to convince Tshombe of their serious opposition. Further US concerns were expressed in response to the news that Tshombe had engaged Jerry Puren, a close friend and Katangan mercenary, to develop an independent Congolese air force, known as 21 Squadron, crewed by South African and Rhodesian pilots who conducted their operations in a singularly aggressive manner. The situation was stabilized when strict restrictions were placed on offensive operations.

The Belgian and US politicians were perturbed by the fact that the advance on Stanleyville and the rescue of American citizens there, including CIA officers, was progressing slower than expected. The directive given to 5 Mechanized Brigade required the force to restore law and order in the eastern provinces. This had changed. 5 Mechanized Brigade was now part of a hostage rescue mission.

On the advice of Colonel Bouzin, the head of the Belgian air force contingent in the Belgian Technical Assistance Group in the Congo, and as a result of Belgian political pressure, Paul Henri Spaak, the Belgian foreign minister, proposed a joint Belgian–American rescue mission to his American counterpart; by 14 November joint planning was underway. The US military planners indicated that the joint planning of rescue operations in the Congo did not imply that the US was predisposed towards this military action. On 15 November, the same day that Dr Carlson was tried and sentenced to death in Stanleyville by the rebels for being a CIA spy, the plan for the rescue operation, referred to as USEUCOM OPLAN 319/64 (United States European Command Operations Plan) or Operation Dragon Rouge was presented to the US Joint Chiefs and both governments for approval.

The operational concept called for a three-stage airborne and air-landed operation aimed at rescuing the hostages in Stanleyville in the shortest possible time in order to minimize the inevitable international political fallout due to the introduction of Western armed forces into an African conflict. The first stage of the operation required 12 US C-130 transport aircraft to fly from their base in France to Kleine Brogel in Belgium, load 545 officers,

NCOs and men of the Belgian Paracommando Regiment, as well as eight armoured jeeps and 12 AS-24 motorized tricycles and fly them 4,134 nautical miles to Ascension Island, a British possession in the South Atlantic. The second stage involved the transportation of the same force east to their staging area at Kamina base in the Katanga province of the Congo and the final preparations for the assault. The last stage would involve the flight north to Basoko, a town approximately 200 kilometres downstream from Stanleyville, from where the force would steer eastward towards the target together with an escort provided by a flight of CIA B-26 aircraft.

The assault on Stanleyville itself was planned to take place in three discreet phases. At 0600 on D-Day 320 members of 1 Parachute Battalion and the Paracommando Regimental HQ would parachute from five C-130s onto the golfcourse adjacent to the Stanleyville airport, then seize and defend the airport and clear it of any obstacles.

Thereafter, two C-130 aircraft, loaded with the eight armoured jeeps, would take off from Kamina and fly directly to Stanleyville, and land on command. Finally, an additional five C-130 aircraft would take off from Kamina and land at Stanleyville, if possible, to deliver one company of 2 Commando Battalion, as well as supplies and spare parts. If a landing was not possible, then the men would parachute onto the airfield and the matériel would be air-dropped. The force was then required to advance into the town, locate hostages, free them, assemble them and return them to the airfield, from where the C-130 aircraft would evacuate them to Leopoldville.

The plan's success hinged on the rapid assault and taking of the airfield in order to allow the aircraft with the armoured jeeps to land. This in turn would provide the force with mobility and additional firepower with which to move rapidly to where the hostages were being held and free them before they could be harmed. The exact location of the hostages was, however, not known.

The review of the plan by both Belgian and especially US military revealed concerns and a debate about who should command the US military component of the operation. The aircraft and support were to be provided by USEUCOM, while combined operations, such as JFT LEO, came under the command of US Strike Command (US STRICOM). This was resolved by inserting a measure into the plan which required the operation to be handed from USEUCOM to US STRICOM once the aircraft had landed at Kamina. General Adams, the Commander in Chief of US STRICOM, voiced his concern that the three passes to be made by the aircraft in order to drop the initial 320 paratroopers onto the drop zone (DZ) from 1,200 feet above ground level would make the paratroops vulnerable to ground fire. He also believed that the movement of the troops by air from Belgium to Kamina via Spain and Ascension Island could not be kept a secret which would eliminate the surprise effect so necessary to achieve success at the Stanleyville objective. The time delay between the enemy sightings of the first paratroopers and the time required to locate and free the hostages was also regarded as the plan's main weakness since the hostages would be at their most vulnerable at this point.

Questions related to the effect of this single operation on the welfare of the hostages and vulnerable Europeans throughout the remainder of rebel-held areas were also voiced. On 18 November, after the Dragon Rouge operation had already commenced, US and Belgian military planners met once again in Brussels to plan additional hostage rescue operations in the other critical cities. The result was a set of three operations, the first of which would begin 48 hours after the completion of Dragon Rouge. Operations Dragon Blanc, Dragon Noir and Dragon Vert were all airborne operations aimed at rescuing and evacuating hostages in Bunia, Paulis and Watsa respectively.

Operation Dragon Rouge

After sustained pressure by the Belgian minister of foreign affairs on his US counterparts to commence the operation and the hesitancy, restrictions and concerns on the part of the latter, 14 USAF C-130 aircraft of 464 Troop Carrier Wing of the USAF, under command of Colonel Burgess Gradwell, took off from Evreux, France and landed at Klein Brogel, Belgium on 17 November 1964, the same day that Colonel Vandewalle was ordered to advance his schedule in order to attack and capture Stanleyville on 23 November. By the next evening all 545 Belgian paracommandos, under the command of Colonel Charles Laurent, an experienced airborne soldier who had parachuted into Stanleyville in 1950 and who had led the paratrooper operation to free Leopoldville in 1960, were on the ground at Ascension Island. The force consisted of a tactical headquarters from the Paracommando Regiment, 1 Paratroop Battalion plus the 12th Company of 2 Commando Battalion, both under command of Major Mine, and a detachment of dispatchers and loadmasters from the Parachute Training Centre under command of Major Ledant. At the same time USAF refuelling vehicles, which would facilitate faster refuelling at the staging area, were dispatched by aircraft to Kamina base. An air photo-reconnaissance mission conducted by a US RC-97 'Running Bear' aircraft succeeded in taking pictures of the DZ and the town of Stanleyville on 16 November but the value of this information came to naught as the intelligence officer tasked to deliver the photos to the force as it transited Spain missed the pickup.

On Ascension Island the USAF members instructed the Belgian paratroopers in jumping techniques from the C-130 aircraft and the radio sets that were to be used during the operation. Other matters discussed and coordinated included the drop procedure to be used to deliver the paratroopers over the drop zone. The DZ location was changed from the golfcourse to the airport itself as a result of these discussions and the assurances given by the US pilots and air force personnel.

An unwanted event ratcheted up the pressure when the operation's cover story was compromised while the main force was still on Ascension Island. This cover story provided for the release of information to the media indicating that US and Belgian forces were conducting a joint long-range airborne training exercise. The story was effectively compromised when a reservist Belgian paratrooper, who happened to be a journalist, was called up for a parade in Brussels and learned that all leave after the parade had been cancelled. The security implications of the failed cover story saw over-flight rights being granted by Spain only minutes before the aircraft entered Spanish airspace, and articles appearing in the *New York Times* on 20 November claiming that US air force planes and Belgian troops were on Ascension Island in order to be readily available to aid hostages in the Congo. The UN secretary-general announced that if such information was correct it could result in action by the UN Security Council. In Stanleyville, however, the effect of the release of information on the joint US-Belgian training exercise appeared to have had little effect.

Tension was also evident between the Belgian military and political planners and their American counterparts over the final decision to attack Stanleyville. The US commanders, used to a tightly controlled decision-making cycle, were aghast when it was discovered that the final decision on the go-ahead for the assault on Stanleyville had been delegated to Colonel Vandewalle, the commander of 5 Mechanized Brigade. This was immediately rescinded and after a number of discussions, an elaborate three-tiered decision-making cycle was instituted instead. In effect, the US had taken over the making and the taking of the final decision on the assault.

Notwithstanding these concerns and tensions, the force took off from Ascension Island after sunset on 21 November and landed safely at Kamina the next day. Here briefings were conducted, JTF LEO members (who represented the hand-over of the control of US forces from EUCOM to STRICOM), Belgian military officers and civilians visited the force and a set of coordinating discussions were held between Colonel Vandewalle and Colonel Laurent. Both commanders agreed that the airborne operation should be carried out on 24 November at 0600 in order to allow a joint assault on Stanleyville by the Dragon Rouge force and 5 Mechanized Brigade, which was closing in on the city from the south. In the interim, members of JTF LEO were indicating that D-Day could be a day earlier and during the evening of 22 November the troops were loaded into the aircraft, only to be unloaded at 0130 the next morning, after no attack order was forthcoming. The opinion of the two assault commanders had eventually held sway.

The order to carry out Operation Dragon Rouge was received during the night of 23/24 November and at 0245 the first five C-130 aircraft, carrying 320 paratroopers, were airborne. With the assistance of the B-26 escort aircraft and a favourable weather report on the cloud cover, the paratroopers arrived over the DZ at 0600. The second and third waves of aircraft, with the armoured jeeps and 12 Company respectively, also took off from Kamina on schedule. Within 80 seconds of their arrival the 320 men had been dispatched from the aircraft at a height of 700 feet above the airfield. Shots were fired at the aircraft from the ground and several aircraft were hit but none was damaged to the extent that

Dragon Rouge commanders, from left: Lieutenants Mertens and Peirlinck, Sergeant Backe, Major Ledant and Colonel Laurent. *Source*: BMA

Moise Tshombe arrives in Stanleyville. *Source*: BMA

they could not continue to carry out their tasks as planned. While the aircraft that had delivered the paratroopers circled the airfield, low cloud drifted in and the airlift commander was forced to orbit at almost treetop level to maintain control of the situation. Eight paratroopers sustained injuries during the jump but only three were unable to participate in the operation.

The HQ Company and the jumpmasters secured the airfield within 30 minutes of landing despite sporadic fire directed at them from the surrounding bush. The other companies moved to silence the rebel gunfire and abandoned machine-gun positions were located around the airfield. Approximately 400 petrol drums, ten wrecked cars and other obstacles were removed from the airstrip and the apron within 15 minutes. The paratroopers also destroyed two of the three vehicles that had tried to flee the airport.

The first aircraft was cleared to land at approximately 0700 and, after having supervised the first landings, the airlift commander, whose aircraft had been damaged by ground fire, flew to Leopoldville. Two aircraft remained on the ground in Stanleyville after all the troops had been delivered and the rest flew on to Leopoldville where they refuelled and waited for the order to commence the evacuation of the hostages.

One of the greatest limitations and uncertainties associated with the operation was the lack of a clear intelligence picture on the location of the hostages and the strength and deployment of the rebels within Stanleyville and its surrounds. The relative strength of the rebels and their most probable course of action according to which they could influence the situation during the hostage rescue operation was, therefore, not easy to discern. This uncertainty, however, changed while the paratroopers were securing the airfield and Colonel Laurent was establishing his tactical headquarters in the control tower. The telephone started ringing in the control tower and an anonymous voice informed the Belgian paracommando officer who answered it that the rescuers should make haste to the Victoria Hotel and the Hotel des Chutes where the hostages were being held. This information was confirmed a few minutes later by a Dutch missionary who

had arrived at the airport to find out what was happening.

A second limitation that had been imposed on the rescue force was the fact that no close air support or air observation had been allocated or approved during the ground operations within Stanleyville. The rationale for this limitation lay in the fear that the rebels would, as in the past, retaliate against their unarmed hostages as a direct result of the delivery of any fire by the B-26 or other ground-attack aircraft. The effect of this limitation was that the forces, once on the ground, were only able to observe as far as they could see themselves.

With the airport under some semblance of control, Phase Three of Operation Dragon Rouge—the rescue of the hostages—commenced. 11 Company, under Captain Emiel Pierlinck and reinforced by two armoured jeeps, was tasked to advance from the airfield to the vicinity of the Victoria Hotel, the Congo Palace and the prison in the centre of the town to locate and free hostages. The company was followed by the Battalion HQ, under Major Mine, and 13 Company, under command of Lieutenant Patte. 13 Company was tasked to follow the main force then turn south, advance on and then take Camp Ketele via the Hotel des Chutes. The paratroopers left the airport at 0715.

The advancing paratroop force was subjected to sporadic small-arms fire from unseen rebel positions along the route into the town but it was only when they reached the built-up area on the western side of the town itself that they were brought under effective machine-gun and small-arms fire, delaying the advance somewhat. Once 11 Company had advanced to within one block of the Victoria Hotel, they heard scattered shots to their south and, on turning the corner into the street within which the Victoria Hotel was located, discovered approximately 250 to 300 hostages huddled in a square. Literally minutes before, the rebels, armed with a collection of approximately six rifles and a number of spears and machetes, had opened fire on the hostages and began stabbing and hacking them. The panicked hostages had fled, leaving two young girls, five women and 15 men, including Dr Carlson, the so-called CIA spy, either dead or dying. Forty hostages, all Belgians, had been wounded, of whom five would later succumb to their

Operation Dragon Noir. The airstrip at Paulis. *Source*: BMA

A paracommando stands guard at Paulis. *Source*: BMA

Dragon Noir commanders, from left: Commandant Holvoet, Colonel Laurent (commander of Dragon Operations) and Major Ledant. *Source*: BMA

wounds. The paratroopers had covered the three kilometres between the airfield and the hotel in approximately 35 minutes and the rebels, on seeing their opponents, had fled.

Members of the battalion headquarters staff and soldiers stabilized the local situation as Major Mine ordered 13 Company to continue towards its three objectives. The civilian casualties were treated on the spot by military medical orderlies and local civilian medical personnel who had arrived to render assistance. Thereafter, they were gathered together in groups of between 100 and 200 under cover from the intermittent rebel fire and by 0830 the first rescued hostages were escorted by the jumpmaster teams in AS-24 tricycles to the airfield for air evacuation. After their evacuation to Leopoldville, they were turned over to their respective national representatives. The severely wounded were transported the three kilometres to the airfield in commandeered civilian vehicles driven by paratroopers. Many additional European civilians, some of whom had been previously wounded or beaten up by the rebels, emerged from hiding places throughout the town and streamed towards the paratroopers and the airfield on foot, desperate to leave with the rescued hostages.

From his command post near the Victoria Hotel, Major Mine directed 11 Company to make haste in locating additional hostages and refugees in order to prevent a repeat of the massacre. 13 Company continued on its route alongside the Congo river

but Major Mine changed the mission of 12 Company, which had arrived at the airport, regrouped and was on its way into the town. Major Mine directed Captain Raes, the company commander, to stop his mission to screen the northern flank of the force and to move to the battalion command post to protect the hostage assembly area. Colonel Laurent, the operation commander, arrived at the battalion command post by AS-24 approximately 30 minutes after the massacre had taken place and reviewed the situation with Major Mine. A platoon of 12 Company was tasked to clear the route back to the airfield as it was coming under increasingly effective harassing fire from the rebels.

11 Company split into its three independent platoons and continued with its original mission, attacking rebels in their area of responsibility, as well as gathering refugees and directing them to the hostage assembly area. Advancing street by street, the company completed its mission by 1300 and took up blocking positions. 11 Company had saved at least another 150 refugees.

13 Company, together with the 4.2-inch mortar platoon, advanced behind 11 Company, then turned south to cover the southern flank of the main effort. Escorted by a Dutch missionary, they reached their first objective, the Procure at the Mission Sacré Coeur. Approximately 50 nuns and missionaries met them, all unharmed, but eager to leave Stanleyville. The group was escorted to the airfield. The company's second objective, the

Evacuees at the airfield at Paulis. *Source*: BMA

Paracommandos packing parachutes in preparation for extraction. *Source:* BMA

Hotel des Chutes, was reached and an additional three refugees and a large amount of arms and ammunition were located. The third objective, Camp Ketele, was next. As the force moved east, they made contact with rebel groups and were also subjected to inaccurate rocket fire but arrived at their target by 0900. The camp was deserted and after securing it, the company, together with the 4.2-inch mortar platoon, established blocking positions in and around the camp itself by 1030. An exchange of fire and grenades continued with a group of rebels located in a village north of the camp, leading to the injury of a paratrooper.

Once the situation in the vicinity of the battalion command post had stabilized, Major Mine directed 12 Company to resume its initial mission to screen the northern flank of the force. Captain Raes and his company departed for the two objectives, namely the native sector of the city known as Belge 1 and Camp Prince Leopold, in order to cut off any rebel infiltration towards the city and the airport. As the company advanced north in two columns, they were subjected to effective rebel fire in the vicinity of the two

stadiums along the routes and another paratrooper was injured. By 1200 the force was ordered to stay in its current location and not to advance farther, a task they continued to pursue until 1600 that day.

The rebels in the vicinity of the airfield had regrouped. A group of 150 rebels had closed in on the western flank of the airfield, while a second group of approximately 180 had occupied the northern border of the strip. The rebels fired on the first two C-130 aircraft filled with refugees at around 0830 as they took off on the flight to Leopoldville, which effectively halted the air evacuation for the next half hour. The firing was eventually reduced through offensive patrols and the evacuation of hostages continued. Sporadic fire was, however, still directed at the aircraft as they came in to land throughout the remaining period of the operation. In due course Belgian foot patrols around the airfield systematically cleared the area. Rebel activity and fire, albeit inaccurate, remained a concern throughout the operation and the Belgian paratroopers did not have the manpower to deal with it conclusively.

Normal loading tables of the C-130 aircraft were largely ignored during the evacuation and up to 120 people were flown out of Stanleyville at a time. Almost 800 people were evacuated on 24 November. Colonel Laurent requested the Belgian embassy to charter additional aircraft to assist with the evacuation effort as the number of refugees and evacuees exceeded the planned airlift capacity of the operation. These aircraft were provided. By late afternoon on 24 November, four T-6, two T-28 and a number of CIA B-26 aircraft had established Stanleyville as their base from which close air support operations were conducted. Stanleyville airfield had become a very busy airfield both in the air and on the ground. The Stanleyville tower was restored to full operational use by 1700 that afternoon.

All Dragon Rouge forces were withdrawn from the city and placed in defensive positions around the airfield by 1815 that evening. A total of approximately 1,400 people had been evacuated by 2100, with another 200 spending the night in a hangar on the airfield itself.

The Link-up between L'Ommegang and the Dragon Rouge Forces

The L'Ommegang force left Lubutu at 1730 on 23 November with the intent to attack and occupy Stanleyville irrespective of whether the Dragon Rouge force had deployed or not. Colonel Vandewalle had decided to undertake a highly risky night advance to cover the remaining distance to the objective as soon as possible in order to be able to achieve this goal. The order of march of the column of nearly 100 vehicles included a vanguard consisting of

A paracommando on picket duty. *Source*: BMA

A C-130 lands at Paulis airfield while Paracommandos look on. *Source*: BMA

Paracommandos return ammunition at Kamina base. *Source*: BMA

Lima 1, with the Ferret armoured cars and the remainder of Mike Hoare's 5 Commando forces, followed by the main force.

At around midnight the lead armoured car reported that a possible enemy vehicle was approaching the column. A 5 Commando rocket-launcher team fired on the suspicious vehicle, setting the stacked arms and ammunition it was carrying alight. An hour later the column ran into a rebel ambush where one member of 5 Commando was killed and a number were wounded. Yet another rebel ambush was triggered an hour later as the column moved towards Stanleyville and a journalist lost his life in the ensuing contact with the rebels. Since there was no doctor allocated to the force the advance continued unabated and medical assistance was provided by medical orderlies as best they could under the circumstances. After the column had encountered a third ambush at approximately 0330 on 24 November, Colonel Vandewalle halted the column and the advance only resumed two hours later as the dawn broke.

Colonel Vandewalle was able to increase the speed of the advance as news of the progress of Operation Dragon Rouge reached him and close air support became available to the column. At the bridge over the Maiko river at Wanie-Rukulu, approximately 60 kilometres from Stanleyville, the force did not stop to clear the scattered rebel positions located on the banks of the river but continued firing at the positions as they crossed the bridge. Similarly, at a distance of approximately 20 kilometres from the town, the lead elements came across groups of vehicles filled with rebels escaping from the Dragon Rouge forces. The close air support and armoured cars brought effective fire to bear on these targets as the column continued its advance. At approximately 1100 on the morning of 24 November the advance elements of L'Ommegang reported visual contact with the blocking-force elements of 13 Company on the eastern outskirts of Camp Ketele. The link-up between the two forces had been achieved.

The L'Ommegang forces deployed into Stanleyville, mostly in accordance with the original plan, and by 1230 the principal escape routes out of Stanleyville had been closed and the strategic bridge over the

Paracommandos emplane for the flight back to Belgium. *Source*: BMA

Parade in Brussels. *Source*: BMA

Tshope river to the north of the city had been occupied by 51 Commando.

Colonel Vandewalle, accompanied by Lieutenant-Colonel Rattan and the CIA members of '58 Commando', proceeded to the airport where they linked up with Major Hardenne, the Dragon Rouge officer responsible for the evacuation of the refugees. The Kitenga canal was designated as the boundary between the L'Ommegang forces and the Dragon Rouge forces, with the latter deploying west thereof by 1700 on 24 November. In the interim, the L'Ommegang forces proceeded to exploit the ground gains to a distance of 45 kilometres around Stanleyville to search for and rescue any additional hostages. Colonel Vandewalle took over control of the city from the Dragon Rouge force at 1700 that day.

Controversy surrounds the operation undertaken to cross the river to the south or left bank to search for and free hostages.

While Mike Hoare contended that the 80-ton river tug *Geri* was in perfect working order in Stanleyville, complete with crew on the day the L'Ommegang forces arrived, others state that the objectives on the south or left bank were supposed to have been taken by the Dragon Rouge forces. Any attempt to cross the river was, however, postponed by Colonel Vandewalle until 27 November, by which time the 28 Belgian priests held hostage near the cathedral had all been killed with the exception of a British woman missionary and her two children. 56 Commando recovered the bodies, after which the rebels closed in again on the south bank.

The L'Ommegang operation had achieved its objective three weeks ahead of its original schedule with the loss of two Belgian officers, three Belgian NCOs, 21 mercenaries and 50 Congolese. Three Belgian officers, three Belgian NCOs, 31 mercenaries and 50 Congolese made up the 87 wounded during the operation. Operation Dragon Rouge had achieved its objective with the loss of one paratrooper killed in action, two wounded in action and three out of action as a result of the jump.

Operation Dragon Noir

The results of Operation Dragon Rouge were still uncertain by the evening of 24 November and the international reaction to the day's military activities was only starting to be felt. The only really good news emanated from a report provided by 52 Commando in the Operation Nord area to the extent that they had successfully taken Aketi and rescued over 100 European hostages without any loss. Third World reaction to the operation was hostile and continued to grow in ferocity as time passed. Sensing the possibility that the political decision-makers would, once again, proceed through a process of exhaustive analysis as to the advantages and disadvantages of conducting the remainder of the planned Dragon operations, the commanders on the ground, including colonels Vandewalle and Laurent, met to discuss the requirements for these operations.

At about the same time the US ambassador in the Congo cabled both the US and Belgian governments with a strong recommendation that the Dragon Rouge forces should be withdrawn to Kamina on 25 November and that on 26 November the operations in Paulis and Bunia should proceed simultaneously. He also stressed that these operations would distance the US and the Belgian forces from any ANC and mercenary retribution

Mortars and aircraft ordnance explode on the left bank at Stanleyville.
Source: Brassinne collection

The battle continues. *Source*: Brassinne collection

meted out in Stanleyville itself. The debriefing of hostages and captured rebels had indicated that the priority regarding the next target should be allocated to Paulis. The rescued Aketi hostages had indicated that a particularly vicious group of rebels held several hundred hostages in Paulis and this conclusion was confirmed by General Mobutu during his visit to the Dragon Rouge forces late on 24 November. Detailed planning for the subsequent Dragon operations started that very evening as the remaining refugees slept in a hangar on the airfield and the exhausted Dragon Rouge paratroopers defended the outer perimeter of the airfield against a possible rebel attack.

On the morning of 25 November a planning meeting was held between colonels Laurent, Isaacson (USAF), Logiest (CAMAC) and the paracommando staffs. A number of factors influenced the tactical planning of the subsequent operations. The paratroopers, most of whom had not been on operations before, were exhausted,

with some troops not having slept for four consecutive nights. The rebels' tenacity and aggression had been underestimated during Operation Dragon Rouge despite the inaccuracy of their fire. The initial plan to attack Paulis (Dragon Noir) and Bunia (Dragon Blanc) simultaneously with a company of paratroopers each was not supported as a result. Thirdly, the number of parachutes available would only allow one more operation. It was concluded that the paracommandos would assault Paulis (Dragon Noir) on the morning of 26 November. It was also confirmed that 5 Mechanized Brigade would not participate in the operation due to the extent of the mopping-up operations underway in and around Stanleyville itself.

The plan called for two paracommando companies to jump from four C-130 aircraft, while three additional C-130s would deliver four armoured jeeps, four radio jeeps and seven AS-24 tricycles to the airstrip once it had been secured. An eighth aircraft would accompany the force and act as a reserve or spare aircraft, as required. D-Day was confirmed as 26 November; 12 aircraft would return to Paulis the next day to evacuate the paracommando force. The political decision-makers in both the US and Belgium agreed with the conclusion and the execution order was given at 0100 on 26 November. Operation Dragon Noir was a go.

The details of the terrain at Paulis were sketchy, but the air reconnaissance photography that had missed the plane in Spain had arrived and was of some assistance to the planners. The town lay approximately 280 kilometres to the northeast of Stanleyville and the airstrip was surrounded by thick woods. The airfield itself was immediately adjacent to the town and its 4,200-foot-long compacted-earth runway, located on the northeastern side of the town, was still usable; the tower and other facilities were located on the southern side of the runway. The town itself had a traffic circle which was critical to any traffic movement along its roads; the European residential area was located to the southwest of the circle. Hotels and business centres were scattered throughout the town and a military base was located to the northwest of the town on the road to Poko, a town some 70 kilometres northwest of Paulis. The airfield was selected as the DZ and it was concluded that the aircraft would have to make multiple passes to dispatch the paratroopers.

The intelligence picture on the rebels and the hostages in Paulis was also sketchy. It was estimated that approximately 300 hostages were in Punia and that the rebels actually expected Bunia to be the next target for any further rescue attempt. It was assumed by the paracommando planning group that the rebels would also have contingency plans in the event of a paracommando drop on Paulis. The lessons learned during Dragon Rouge were also taken into

5 Commando crosses the river to the left bank to look for hostages. *Source*: Brassinne collection

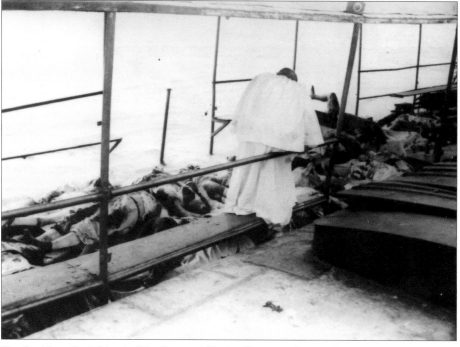

The dead from the left bank of the Congo at Stanleyville return. *Source*: Brassinne collection

passes at first light on 26 November. 11 Company would land, assemble and move into the town immediately to locate and gather any hostages. 13 Company would land, assemble, clear the runway of any obstacles and then hold the airfield for the duration of the operation. Independent reconnaissance operations would be conducted by the reconnaissance section and the jumpmasters while 12 Company would remain in Stanleyville as the operational reserve.

The air crews earmarked for the Dragon Noir operation had returned to Leopoldville and, just as in the case of the paracommandos, were suffering from fatigue. Aircraft maintenance and repair tasks were required but the air crews were unfortunately also capitulating to severe attacks of diarrhoea and vomiting. Notwithstanding this, the complexities of staging at the over-extended Stanleyville airfield and the navigation challenges to locate the DZ at Paulis, all the aircraft arrived at Stanleyville in good order.

At a final coordination meeting between participants it was discovered that the Belgian and USAF planning for the approach direction to the DZ differed by 180 degrees. The Belgians wanted a west–east approach, while the USAF favoured the opposite. Tensions increased between the two allies and the direction of the final approach was only resolved in favour of the Belgians as the aircraft approached Paulis itself. The first aircraft took off from Stanleyville at 0500 on 26 November and on the first low-level pass over the DZ at Paulis an hour later the aircraft were subjected to anti-aircraft fire emanating from the airport buildings to the south of the airstrip. The aircraft stopped the drop on the first pass and warned pilots to avoid the buildings.

account and the paracommandos were tasked to jump with battle kit only, to group as quickly as possible once they had landed and to advance into the town on foot thereafter without waiting for the armoured jeeps to land. The use of the B-26 aircraft in the close air support role was debated once again and the paracommandos recommended that they should not be used for fear that the rebels would retaliate by killing hostages. Colonel Gradwell, the USAF commander, resisted this recommendation and the aircraft remained available for close air support as a consequence.

Orders for Operation Dragon Noir were conveyed to the paracommandos at 1700 on 25 November. Four C-130 aircraft were to drop 240 troops over the DZ at Paulis airfield in three

The formation came around and the drop began on the second pass over the DZ. The aircraft were subjected to intense ground fire and several were hit in the process. The foggy weather, which had caused the B-26 escort aircraft to lose their way, acted to the advantage of the paracommandos and they were largely screened as they descended.

Once on the ground, 13 Company assaulted the control tower and silenced the anti-aircraft machine gun and by 0630 the airfield had been cleared for landing. Further actions were undertaken

Bewildered, Stanleyville. *Source*: Brassinne collection

thereafter to secure the perimeter and prepare for the evacuees.

On landing, 11 Company assembled speedily and move directly into the town to the west of the airfield where each of the three platoons peeled off to undertake their respective missions: rescue at the mission station by 1 Platoon, a blocking action to prevent any interference from the military camp by 2 Platoon and a search of the residential area by 3 Platoon.

Reaching the mission station at 0700, 1 Platoon managed to rescue 50 hostages, after having picked up and escorted scattered refugees along the way and routed them to the airfield with the help of commandeered vehicles. 2 Platoon ran from their assembly area to the designated blocking position and held it successfully despite being subjected to enemy fire until they withdrew later in the day. 3 Platoon ran from their assembly area on the airfield into the centre of town to rescue the women and children who were reportedly holed up in the Hotel Mangreth. This information proved to be unfounded and they were ordered to move to and occupy the town's central traffic circle. Under heavy fire from rebels in houses adjacent to their advance route the platoon incurred one fatality and a number of men were wounded. By 0900 the paracommandos had gathered in excess of 200 people, who were screened in order to obtain information on the possible location of other refugees in the town. Once this information had been obtained, the reconnaissance section and the jumpmasters were sent on missions to locate and

direct the new evacuees to the airfield. Paracommando patrols were probing as far as eight kilometres from the airfield as the day progressed.

The deployed platoons remained in their assigned area of responsibility searching for hostages and refugees until 1600 hours, whereupon they withdrew to the airfield. One soldier had died in contact and five had been wounded. The two companies established a smaller perimeter around the western end of the airfield and together with the refugees that had been collected during the day, settled down to wait for the evacuation aircraft to arrive the next day.

The evacuation of refugees and the withdrawal of the paracommandos commenced at 1200 on 27 November in spite of information which indicated that more hostages were being held approximately 40 kilometres from the town. By 1610 the last aircraft had taken off from Paulis and Operation Dragon Noir had ended. The paracommandos had succeeded in rescuing 375 refugees and hostages within 36 hours, for the loss of one soldier and five others wounded. More than 20 hostages had been killed in Paulis by the rebels and, as the last aircraft left Paulis airspace, the rebels reclaimed the town.

The Fallout

An international political firestorm erupted as the exhausted Dragon forces and USAF personnel were being extracted from their various locations and regrouped at Kamina base. Demonstrations took place in Nairobi, Cairo, Moscow, Prague and Peking and widespread negative press coverage was circulated throughout the world. Thus, in spite of the efforts and pleas of the diplomatic community in Leopoldville for the Dragon forces to undertake the remaining two rescue operations in Bunia (Operation Dragon Blanc) and Watsa (Operation Dragon Vert) respectively, the political decision to withdraw the paracommandos was communicated to the Belgian and US embassies in Leopoldville by the US secretary of state Dean Rusk at 1700 on 26 November 1964.

Colonel Laurent's forces completed their extraction to Kamina base and the flight home to Belgium via Ascension Island and Las Palmas commenced on 28 November 1964. The last aircraft landed in Belgium two days later. The paracommandos received a rapturous welcome in Brussels, medals were awarded to the commanders by the king and the troops paraded through the city streets to the delight of the general public.

The media, after a check with the various embassies in the Congo, calculated that there were still as many as 900 foreign nationals unaccounted for within the rebel-held areas in the east of the country. The Dragon operations were over but the war against the rebels was not.

CHAPTER SEVEN:
PACIFICATION OPERATIONS IN THE EASTERN PROVINCES

A Ugandan POW (centre) captured inside the Congo.
Source: Vandewalle Collection

Adjudant, later Lieutenant, Bouve, a Belgian mercenary (pictured earlier), was attached to 5 Commando during Operation White Giant.
Source: Brassinne collection

The Military Situation at the End of 1964

A changed military situation faced Colonel Vandewalle once the paracommandos had returned to Belgium and 5 Mechanized Brigade had reoccupied the old 3 Command Headquarters building in the centre of Stanleyville.

In Stanleyville itself the battle for control of the urban area continued unabated and Colonel Vandewalle estimated that he would require another three weeks before the town, including the left bank, could be secured. By the end of the year the commercial areas of Stanleyville had been looted three times: by the mercenaries, then the ANC and thereafter by the local civilian population; the empty streets were littered with destroyed vehicles, refuse and shattered glass. The physical damage to Stanleyville was less far-reaching than the economic collapse brought about by the evacuation of the 2,000 skilled and semi-skilled Europeans during Operation Dragon Rouge. These maladies paled into insignificance when compared to the acts of violence, even cannibalism, committed by ANC solders as they cleared the large black residential areas in Stanleyville of possible rebel concentrations.

On 18 December, 5 Commando, in a wide sweep of the towns adjacent to Stanleyville, reached Banalia, only to find it deserted. From the identity documents and bloodstained clothing found at the ferry crossing over the Aruwimi river, it was concluded that 16 Europeans had been killed at the landing and their bodies cast into the river. The town of Bafwasende, northeast of Stanleyville, was retaken on 19 December and the bodies of 14 Europeans were discovered. Farther northeast, Wamba fell to 54 Commando ten

days later and 30 European bodies were discovered, while the mercenaries discovered ten victims on 30 December at Mungbere. Harrowing tales also emerged of the massacre of 30 Europeans in Watsa, the target of the cancelled Operation Dragon Vert, while the paracommandos were at Paulis.

In the operational area farther afield the Operation Kivu force, led by 53 Commando, reached Bunia, the target of the cancelled Operation Dragon Blanc, and freed 122 European hostages and 47 ANC soldiers. A nun and three priests had been murdered by the rebels and almost every captured ANC soldier had been tortured and mutilated. Paulis, the target of Operation Dragon Noir, had been recaptured by the rebels and, more importantly, Punia, located on the main surface supply route from Kamina to Stanleyville had fallen into rebel hands once again. All in all it was estimated that by the end of 1964 the rebels had killed 300 Europeans in the eastern areas of the Congo and that approximately 1,000 Europeans living throughout the eastern provinces were still in danger of attack.

The large number of vulnerable Europeans still left to their own devices stunned and angered observers outside the Congo, and the US and Belgian governments were roundly condemned for sacrificing the remaining hostages in order to appease world opinion. There was also a school of military thought which claimed that the Belgian paracommandos did indeed still have the capacity to carry out the last two planned operations against Bunia and Watsa. In the face of the negative public reaction against the Dragon operations, a viable option with which to maintain and

Mercenaries and ANC enter Mahagi.
Source: Vandewalle collection

Chris Craft P boats manned by 5 Commando's *Force Navale* on Lake Tanganyika. *Source*: Iain Peddle

The modified trawler, *Ermans*, was captained by Iain Peddle and armed with a variety of heavy weapons, including a 75mm recoilless rifle. *Source*: Iain Peddle.

The Greek crew of *Ermans*.
Source: Iain Peddle

further US and Belgian interests in the Congo was sought, and found, in the integration of mercenaries into ANC units and their utilization as independent units on specific tasks.

The recruitment of mercenaries was, however, no longer that simple. The 111 Belgian officers and NCOs who had made a major contribution to the L'Ommegang effort started to rotate out of the Congo back to Belgium on 22 December and a valuable source of experience and expertise was lost. The men of 5 and 6 Commandos, the two most prominent mercenary units during the L'Ommegang operations, were also nearing the end of their six-month contracts and, in an effort to retain their expertise, General Mobutu promoted Mike Hoare to the rank of lieutenant-colonel and offered to extend the mercenaries' contracts. Only ten enlisted for the next six months and a period of recruitment throughout South Africa and Rhodesia and training at Kamina was required before the reconstituted 5 Commando was battle-ready. Lieutenant-Colonel Lamouline, the Belgian commander of Lima II during the L'Ommegang operations, was appointed as the officer

commanding 6 Commando and a similar process of recruitment in Europe and training in the Congo followed.

The Counterinsurgency Plan

The intelligence gathered on the rebels in the eastern provinces of the Congo indicated that they still controlled the areas outside the main towns. A number of towns in the Oriental province, as well as the Fizi–Baraka area of Kivu province, were also still under their control. In addition, the rebels were supported by the local population in ANC-controlled towns, including Stanleyville, Pontiersville, Opala, Basoko, and Kasongo and Kambare in South Kasai province. None of the rebel leaders had been captured as yet. The options available to the rebels were assessed by the intelligence staff and it was concluded that they would probably attempt to recapture Stanleyville in order to exploit the propaganda value of such a victory. In addition, they would attempt to maintain their current areas of influence and extend their area of operations west from the mountainous Fizi–Baraka pocket to sever the main

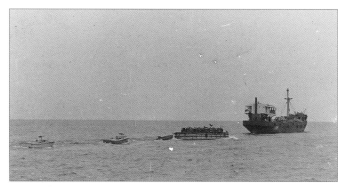

Operation Banzi. Invasion fleet on the way to Baraka.
Source: Iain Peddle

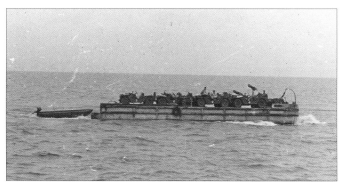

Jeeps on the invasion barge.
Source: Iain Peddle

supply route between Kamina and Stanleyville. The neighbouring countries of Uganda, Sudan and Tanzania were all channelling arms, ammunition, vehicles and supplies to the rebels and control of the northeastern region of Orientale province and the crossings over Lake Tanganyika were vital to them as a consequence.

On 15 December 1964 Colonel Vandewalle issued 5 Mechanized Brigade operations order No. 6 to give effect to this strategy. The operations order emphasized that the 52 Belgian officers and NCOs due to arrive in the Congo via CAMAC would no longer be conducting offensive operations and that their role was to provide staff and other support within the larger ANC units and headquarters. The mission of the ANC forces in the rebel areas (including the Operation Nord, Operation Tshuapa and Operation Kivu areas) was to hold conquered territory, to reorganize and then to pacify the rebel areas. The concept of operations indicated that the ANC and the mercenaries would be required to occupy the main towns to deny them to the rebels, keep strong garrison forces at Stanleyville and Kindu, hold the Paulis and Bunia plains and seal the borders with Uganda, Sudan and the Central African Republic, and cut the insurgents' supply chain by capturing the Fizi–Baraka pocket and patrolling Lake Tanganyika.

Protecting the Towns and Main Supply Routes

The occupation and domination of towns and areas held by government forces was largely allocated to ANC units, including those formed from former Katangan units. Sub-units of 6 Commando, known as *chocs* or shock units, were allocated to each unit to strengthen leadership, planning and support functions. In Stanleyville itself, the town and the left bank were garrisoned under command of Lieutenant-Colonel Itambo of the ANC, who had both 11 and 14 Katanga Commandos under his command, as well as the civilian and military police. Public order policing, the occupation of the town and the protection of the ammunition dump were within his purview. Kindu, on the main commercial and supply route between Stanleyville and the south, was occupied by battalions, and a platoon of mercenaries was also deployed to bolster the capability of the force. Farther south, the town of Kongolo was garrisoned as well and strengthened by a platoon of mercenaries. 10 Commando, under command of Major Jean Schramme, was tasked to conduct mopping-up operations in Kambare and Kasongo. Albertville and Lulimba were garrisoned by four battalions as well as members of 6 Commando and the

defence of the border region between Bukavu and Bunia was allocated to an ANC battalion. The remaining Operation Nord forces, excluding the previously allocated 5 Commando members, were tasked with the defence of Paulis, Bambessa and Poko, while the Operation Tshuapa forces, also minus their mercenaries, were tasked with the defence of the airfield at Ikele.

The return of traffic on the Congo river to its former levels between Bumba and Stanleyville was achieved relatively quickly and efficiently in January 1965, not least through the efforts of an enterprising Belgian paratroop officer. The escort force was under the command of Second Lieutenant Michal Neyt, a paratroop officer who had been allocated to 5 Mechanized Brigade Headquarters in Stanleyville as an intelligence officer and commander of the 4.2-inch mortar platoon during the rotation of Belgian troops. Tasked to re-open the vital river traffic over the 400 kilometres between Bumba and Stanleyville, he was charged with escorting three towboats, each pushing four barges, one tugboat and one sonar vessel. He deployed one platoon from 1 Paratroop Battalion (ANC) on each tow-barge vessel, with a command post on the leading tow-barge and a total of 18 mercenaries from the Bero Platoon of 6 Commando on the leading sonar vessel and the tug. In an innovative utilization of the available materials at his disposal, Neyt used bags of salt as protection for his 81mm mortar on board one of the vessels. The operation lasted three days and the 12 barges delivered much needed commodities with which to sustain the Stanleyville population. The river had been re-opened.

Operation White Giant

While the deployment of garrison forces gave effect to the requirement to hold the existing territory within the government's control, the offensive component of the strategy required a different approach. An independent mobile strike force capable of offensive actions was required.

Early in 1965 General Mobutu established Operation North-East, a new operational area alongside the border with Sudan and Uganda in the Orientale province, and placed it under command of the newly promoted Lieutenant-Colonel Mike Hoare. He was required to seal off the border areas with Uganda and Sudan with the two infantry battalions under his command. All available air support would be provided to support the force as well. Operation North-East would establish its headquarters at Bunia and would

Jeeps and 5 Commando troops on the invasion barge. *Source*: Iain Peddle

report to Lieutenant-Colonel Noel, the Chief of Staff to Colonel Mulamba, the ANC commander at 3 Command Headquarters in Stanleyville.

The forces gathered to give effect to the Operation North-East mission consisted of the reconstituted 5 Commando, comprising 270 men organized into eight commandos, one armoured car troop equipped with Ferret armoured cars, one mortar platoon; and 14 Commando, an ANC infantry battalion of 700 largely Katangan soldiers, commanded by Lieutenant-Colonel Tavernier, a Belgian mercenary. The force composition gave effect to the requirement for a strike force, together with an occupation force, to return captured areas to government administration once the strike force had moved on to its next objective.

The first action undertaken by 5 Commando was aimed at securing the Ugandan border. Operation Kingfisher, combined with an advance by both battalions north from Bunia to Mahagi and Mahagi Port on Lake Albert, commenced on 15 March 1965 with this objective in mind. The Operation Kingfisher force, consisting of 58 and 59 Commandos, embarked on a number of fishing vessels on Lake Albert, with the objective of striking Port Mahagi in a seaborne assault. The remainder of the force, Force Whisky, advanced along the main route to Mahagi, with a view to attacking it simultaneously with the seaborne assault. The early progress along the advance route was hampered by contacts with the rebels, 5 Commando casualties and poor radio communications. Notwithstanding these initial mishaps, the ground force took

Mahagi and elements thereof turned east to assist the Kingfisher force which had landed successfully and occupied Port Mahagi. Both forces were, however, brought under fire from rebels and members of the Ugandan National Army from the Ugandan side of the border, resulting in a number of firefights across this international border. Approximately 200 rebels had escaped to the relative safety of Uganda and evidence of Ugandan support for the rebels was confirmed by the capture and repatriation of a Ugandan soldier. 14 Commando forces occupied the objectives, while 100 local men sympathetic to the ANC were recruited to assist as guides and scouts. The start line and right flank for the first phase of Operation White Giant had been secured.

Operation White Giant was launched to capture Aru and Aba on the Ugandan and Sudanese borders respectively, as well as Faradje, a centre on the main route, located approximately 100 kilometres from the Sudanese border. The first phase of the offensive involved taking Aru, which was achieved after a number of smaller objectives, including villages and bridges, along the route had been cleared of rebel presence during short, sharp contacts. Captured arms and equipment indicated that the rebels were increasingly being armed with AK-47 rifles and Chinese heavy machine guns. Information received and captured documents confirmed that the Ugandan National Army was actively engaged in providing ammunition to the rebels in exchange for ivory and gold from the mine at Watsa.

Leaving 14 Commando to defend Aru, 5 Commando advanced on Aba, the headquarters of the rebels in the Orientale province and

Smoke rises from the beachhead at Baraka. *Source*: Iain Peddle

5 Commando troops on *Ermans*. *Source*: Iain Peddle

The bunkers dug in at Baraka. *Source*: Iain Peddle

the town through which aid from Sudan was channelled. The target was attacked on foot and, after a short skirmish on the outskirts, the rebel headquarters was captured. Seven 76mm recoilless rifles, a number of grenade launchers and an Algerian 120mm mortar were found, together with evidence of a Sudanese and Egyptian presence and support for the rebels. A key bridge on the road between Aba and the Sudanese border was destroyed by members of 5 Commando, as was a bridge between Aru and Uganda, thus sealing off the northeast of the Congo from any access by wheeled vehicles. The town of Faradje, located 65 kilometres inland from Aba, was attacked the next day at sunset by a mobile force consisting of 54 Commando, the mortar platoon and three companies of 14 Commando. The forces consolidated their position in Aba and Faradje while the next phase of the operation was planned.

The aim of the second phase of Operation White Giant was to recapture the remaining large towns in the Orientale province and to restore government administration and basic services to the surrounding areas. The targets included the gold-mining town of Watsa, south of Faradje, whose riches had helped finance the rebellion. The bridge over the Kibali river, north of Watsa, was regarded by both sides as the key terrain associated with the defence of Watsa. With the support of CIA B-26 and T-28 aircraft the key ground around the Kibali bridge at Watsa was assaulted and the rebels withdrew from the bridge and the town. Four Europeans, whose skills had been needed to continue the production of the gold mine, were located; they informed the mercenaries that the remaining 38 Belgians in the town had been shot out of hand by the rebels.

The last towns in the Operation North-East area that were still under rebel control included Dungu, Niangara and Gombari. 5 Commando was given the task of recapturing these centres. Gombari, to the southwest of Watsa, was re-occupied by 14 Commando with 5 Commando support and the force now concentrated its efforts westward on the remaining two main centres of rebel activity. The deserted town of Gangala, east of Faradje, was taken by the force, whereafter Dungu and Niangara fell on successive days to the overwhelming firepower of the 100-strong 5 Commando sub-unit commonly referred to as Force John-John, under command of Captain John Peters. The civilian population was encouraged to return to the town and, in a repeat of previous successes, 5 Commando succeeded in restoring the government administration in the areas it occupied. The 5 Commando rear headquarters at Bunia was closed down and moved to Faradje in preparation for the next phase of pacification operations. The closure of the border with Sudan and Uganda had taken a mere seven weeks to achieve.

Operation Violettes Imperiales

The momentum achieved by the success of Operation White Giant was not lost on the planners at 3 Command Headquarters in Stanleyville and in short shift a plan for Operation Violettes Imperiales was completed. The offensive involved the seizure of Buta and Bondo, both towns which were important to rebel support routes from Sudan and the Central African Republic respectively. 5 Commando was tasked to advance 630 kilometres west from Faradje and take Bili and Buta, while 6 Commando was required to advance from Paulis, seize Poko and attack Buta at the same time as 5 Commando.

After 5 Commando's headquarters had been moved to Niangara, the operation commenced on 29 May 1965. The order of battle included 110 men from 5 Commando, including mortarmen, an ANC bridging unit and two armoured cars. After a successful advance without many incidents, the 5 Commando force crossed the Bomakandi river and attacked Bili. The town was deserted but there was evidence that the two Norwegian missionaries who had been held captive in the town had been hastily evacuated by the rebels as they withdrew ahead of the 5 Commando attack. During the night the rebels rode into a 5 Commando ambush and, after one of their vehicles had escaped, they counter-attacked and killed one mercenary. Bili had, however, been secured.

The 188-kilometre advance on Bondo was completed and 5 Commando, unsure of the deployment of the rebels, lay up overnight, intending to attack the town at daylight the following day. During the night, however, the rebels withdrew from the town, taking their hostages with them. On 1 June, 5 Commando was ordered by 3 Command Headquarters to abandon Bondo and move at best speed south to Buta. This movement involved a combat crossing over the Likati river, where evidence of the mass killings of European hostages was found. Both 5 and 6 Commandos reached Buta within an hour of each other, but there were no signs of any hostages. A Swiss man appeared out of the bush to confirm that 38 priests had been led to the bridge over the Rubi river the previous evening and all had been killed. Their bodies had been dumped in the water.

With the towns secured, civil administration services restored and surviving hostages rescued, 5 Commando operations began to wind down in the Operation North-East area and the contracts of many of the men ended. Mike Hoare was once again requested by General Mobutu to renew his contract in order to assist in the re-capture of the Fizi–Baraka pocket adjacent to Lake Tanganyika in the Kivu province.

Operation South and Che Guevara

The retaking of the Fizi–Baraka pocket as expressed in the 5 Mechanized Brigade operations order of 15 December 1964 was proving to be more difficult than initially anticipated and a new operational area, referred to as Operation South, was established to enable a focused effort at achieving the objective. The area stretched north from Albertville to Uvira and to Bukavu, then west and southwest to include the towns of Mwenga, Kalole, Wamaza, Kasongo, Kongolo, and finally Nyunzu. Colonel Kakudji (ANC) was appointed as the officer commanding Operation South, with Lieutenant-Colonel Roger Hardenne, a Belgian paratrooper who had participated in the Dragon operations, as his Chief of Staff. The headquarters of Operation South was established at Albertville on Lake Tanganyika and planning for an offensive against the rebels during the second half of 1965 commenced.

The area in question was situated adjacent to the western shores of Lake Tanganyika and included mountainous areas, such as the Mitumba mountain range, with elevations of up to 10,000 feet. The region where the rebels were active stretched 240 kilometres from Kabimba, north of Albertville, to Uvira on the northern shores of the lake to Kabimba, and 260 kilometres inland as far as Kasongo.

The rebels in the designated area, referred to as the APL 'Eastern Front', were led by Laurent Kabila, a former pro-Lumumba Balubakat rebel who had fought against Moise Tshombe during the Katangan secession. His supporters were drawn from the Bahembi tribe, a traditionally hostile local tribe, as well as Rwandan rebels sympathetic to his cause. The rebel cause was strengthened on 23 April when Che Guevara, the Cuban revolutionary, crossed Lake Tanganyika from Kigoma, entered the Congo at Kibamba and set up a mountain headquarters at Luluabourg close to the lake. As many as 120 Afro-Caribbean Cubans followed him over the next seven months to assist the rebels on the Eastern Front against the government. Cubans were also detached to Kibamba to assist with incoming logistics from Kigoma across Lake Tanganyika, the rebel base at Makungu and Rwandan forces based at Bendera.

Operations order No. 1 promulgated by Operation South Headquarters provided for a three-phase offensive to be conducted against the Eastern Front of the rebels (APL) by 5 Commando, with the *Force Navale* (Naval Force) under operational control, 5 Infantry Battalion (ANC), 9 Commando, the Kongolo Battalion, 14 Infantry Battalion (ANC) and a company of 8 Battalion (ANC). Air support was to be provided by eight T-28 and two B-26 aircraft as well as a Bell 47 helicopter and a DC-3 Dakota.

The naval force in question consisted of six Chris Craft P boats provided by the US, armed with machine guns, manned by members of 5 Commando and utilized on interdiction missions on Lake Tanganyika and a converted trawler, the *Ermans*, which was armed with a 75mm recoilless rifle and a number of .50 inch Browning machine guns, plus an assortment of other light machine guns and captured weapons. Captained by Iain Peddle, the vessel

CIA B-26 Invader light attack bombers.
Source: Brassinne collection

CIA T-28 aircraft.
Source: Brassinne collection

was destined to play an important role in military operations along the lakeshore. The offensive capacity of the naval forces on Lake Tanganyika was also greatly enhanced through the provision of a number of armed Swift boats, provided by the US and manned by on-side Cubans. During operations a tug and an assortment of barges were also requisitioned from the cement factory operation and port at Kabimba, 48 kilometres north of Albertville.

The mission of Operation South was to destroy all rebel forces in the designated area of operations in three phases. Phase One required the rebels to be cleared from the coastal areas from Albertville north to Baraka by three battalions, while key areas such as Albertville and Kabambare and the railway line into the interior were to be protected. The second phase provided for the clearance of the coastal area and the adjacent areas farther north to Uvira and Mwenga respectively, while a third offensive would target Pene-Mende farther inland. The final phase of the offensive involved the clearance of the Ruzizi river valley north to Bukavu as well as the destruction of the enemy situated north of Kabambare.

Mike Hoare had again been persuaded to extend his service as the officer commanding 5 Commando. He set about recruiting and training a further intake of South African and Rhodesian mercenaries to man the forces defending and administering the towns in the Operation North-East sector along the Aru–Niangara arc in the Orientale province, as well as establishing a 350-man battalion of infantry and a naval force to conduct operations against the rebels in the Fizi–Baraka pocket with effect from September 1965.

In the interim, the first documented contact between the Cubans who flew for the CIA air force in support of the government and Che Guevara's Cubans occurred on 19 June. Local inhabitants had informed intelligence sources in the area that a rebel camp had been established in the vicinity of Yungu on the coastline. Two B-26 and four T-28 aircraft flown by the Cuban members of CIA took off from Albertville airport and strafed the camp, whereupon the fire was returned by a 12.7mm anti-aircraft machine gun, in violation of Che Guevara's strict orders to the contrary. Neither side knew of the other's existence or the fact that they had engaged in conflict with fellow nationals until intelligence reports revealed

this much later.

The presence of the Cuban forces in the Fizi–Baraka area become known on 29 June when a dead Cuban soldier was found after a combined rebel, Rwandan and Cuban attack on the ANC forces guarding the hydroelectric power station at Bendera and the village of Katenga. Items of clothing found on the dead Cuban were made in Cuba, and the soldier's diary confirmed this. Guevara's diary of events also indicates that four Cubans and 14 Rwandans were killed during the failed attack. Che Guevara's presence among the Cubans in the area was, however, not known to the Congolese, Belgian or US intelligence sources.

The Cuban intervention in the Congo on the rebel side was beset with problems as Guevara's more traditional guerrilla-warfare approach to the local population was stridently opposite to the exploitation meted out by the rebels, whom he regarded as ill-disciplined and uncommitted to the cause. The lack of success, the increased pressure brought to bear on the rebels and the Cubans by the Congolese forces and mercenaries and the resulting tension between them were cited as contributory factors to Che Guevara's decision to accept that the mission had failed; he abandoned the effort in November 1965.

Operation Banzi

The first phase of the Operation South campaign commenced on 27 September 1965 with 5 Commando's seaborne assault on the coastal settlement of Baraka by Force John-John, under command of Major Peters, and Force Oscar under command of Captain Hugh van Oppen, supported by a simultaneous attack towards Fizi from Lulimba by Force Alpha under command of Major Alistair Wicks. The main attack came up against a determined and well-organized defence and it took two days before the beachhead could be secured. Force Alpha's supporting attack was halted in the vicinity of Lubonja by a number of well-prepared defensive and delaying positions laid by the rebels. Force Alpha was withdrawn from this position and, together with two companies of Congolese soldiers and heavy equipment, was ferried up the lake to join and reinforce the main force in Baraka. It took until 9 October for 5 Commando to wrest control of Baraka from the rebels, after which they advanced on Fizi, leaving the two Congolese companies to occupy the town. Captured documents provided information on the location of rebel concentrations which proved useful in subsequent operations. The town of Fizi fell to 5 Commando on 13 October and was handed over to 9 Commando. Thereafter, the focus of the operation was southward, with Makungu taken a week later. 5 Commando then took Kasimia in a combined land–sea assault on 19 October and the Yungu bases were overrun by ANC forces a day later.

Rebel activity spread to the west of the lake and to the south, forcing the ANC forces to Kongolo and Niemba and an additional effort was required to defend against attacks on railway lines surrounding Albertville. Operation South reorganized its forces and in February 1966 a systematic clearing of rebel bases and pacification was undertaken, enabling Phase One of the offensive to be declared a success by the end of March.

Phase Two of the Operation South operations order No. 1 commenced in April. 5 Commando, now under command of Major Peters, advanced north along the lake towards Uvira, while elements of 6 Commando and 5 Infantry Battalion (ANC) advanced on a parallel axis to their west. After two months of

operations against the rebels, the headquarters of Operation South declared that the situation was such that Phase Three of the campaign could commence. 5 Commando, together with 9 Commando, two shock units (platoons) of 6 Commando and 8 and 13 Infantry Battalions regrouped in Uvira and advanced north along the Ruzizi river valley towards Bukavu, while 5 Infantry Battalion and an element of 6 Commando crested the escarpment south of Mwenge and married up with the ANC garrison forces in Mwenge.

The areas adjacent to the Pene-Mende–Wamaza–Kongolo road and its associated villages were still firmly under rebel control and the local support for the rebels was strong. On 14 July the headquarters of Operation South instructed units in the area to give effect to a plan to isolate the rebels and pacify the surrounding area. This plan, referred to as the new Phase Four of the Operation South campaign, was unfortunately not effected due to the requirement for troops to be deployed to counter the revolt of the Katangan Baka Regiment in Stanleyville. It had taken almost a year for the Operation South forces to destroy the rebels and reclaim the sovereignty of this operational area.

CHAPTER EIGHT:
THE MERCENARY REBELLION

General Mobutu's Coup d'État

On 13 October 1965, the very day that 5 Commando was securing Fizi, political instability returned to the Congo when President Kasavubu relieved Prime Minister Tshombe of his duties and replaced him with Evarista Kimba. A period of intense instability followed until on 24 November 1966 when the newly promoted Lieutenant-General Mobutu, with tacit CIA support, relieved both President Kasavubu and Prime Minister Kimba of their powers and took over the presidency. Lieutenant-Colonel Leonard Mulamba was appointed as the new prime minister and Major-General Bobozo was promoted and appointed as the head of the ANC.

Moise Tshombe had been widely regarded as a personal friend and sponsor of both 5 and 6 Commandos and so this event cast a pall of uncertainty over the future of the mercenaries in the Congo. Jerry Puren, a mercenary from the Katangan secession period and long-time adviser to Tshombe, left with Tshombe into exile in Belgium. Mike Hoare and Alistair Wicks did not renew their contracts and left the Congo. Major John Peters, the new officer commanding 5 Commando, pledged and demonstrated his and the unit's loyalty to the government cause by continuing to conduct operations in the Operation South area until the unit was disbanded in April 1967. Belgian officers in a variety of positions in the military in the Congo, including Colonel Vandewalle, Colonel Lamouline and Major Protin, also all left the Congo after their contracts ended. 6 Commando, now under command of Bob Denard, had sub-units deployed throughout

the area north of Stanleyville, as well as in the Operation South area. 10 Commando, under command of Jean Schramme and headquartered in Punia, had established a form of independent military and political control over the Maniema region of the Kivu province.

The First Revolt

Once in Belgium, Jerry Puren obtained access to a plan whose aim it was to reinstall Tshombe as the prime minister. The conspirators indicated to him that in addition to the Baka Regiment, Jean Schramme and Bob Denard had pledged their support for the plan. Puren believed that the plan was not viable and refused to take part. Mike Hoare, Alistair Wicks, John Peters and Hugh van Oppen, all former or serving members of 5 Commando, were said to have been approached with a view to supporting the proposed uprising. All refused their support. There are indications that Hugh van Oppen, in line to succeed Lieutenant-Colonel Peters as the next commander of 5 Commando, agreed to support the rebellion and was killed on 13 May 1966 as a result. The truth of this matter is still shrouded in mystery.

On 23 July Katangan troops of the Baka Regiment in Stanleyville—11, 12, 13 and 14 Commandos, each commanded by French, German and Belgian mercenary officers—revolted in support of the exiled Moise Tshombe, killed the commander of the ANC and took over the radio station. In the confusion Bob Denard, whose 6 Commando forces were deployed in and around Stanleyville, seized the banks and the post office. Denard then

Jean Schramme, commander of 10 Commando, at Manono garrison, October 1964. *Source*: J.P. Sonck collection

Major Bob Denard, commander of 6 Commando (left), with Colonel Noël, Chief of Staff of 5 Brigade. *Source*: Noël via J.P. Sonck

Members of 57 Commando in the Operation South area. *Source*: James MacKenzie collection

contacted President Mobutu, informing him that a mutiny was underway in Stanleyville and demanded that General Mulamba, the prime minister, travel to Stanleyville to negotiate with the plotters. The situation reached a stalemate, with Denard holding the communications and the banks, the Katangans holding the airfield and the prime minister trying to negotiate a solution. Denard's actual position in this uprising— plotter or opportunist—has never really been clarified.

Attempts were made to resolve the stalemate and Commandant Wautier, the commander of 11 Commando (Katangan) was killed in Stanleyville while attempting to convince members of 6 Commando to join the rebellion. 14 Commando, in the interim, under command of Major Wilhelm, advanced on and took Paulis from the ANC, before advancing on Stanleyville with the aim of taking it. His force, however, drove into a rebel ambush on the way. Sixty Katangans and ten mercenaries were killed and the commander fatally wounded. The remainder of 14 Commando, now under command of 'Frenchie' Delamichel, did not reach Stanleyville until 15 August.

The situation in Stanleyville was stalemated until September when Denard suddenly attacked the Katangans deployed in the city. Units involved in the final phases of Operation South, including 5 Commando, had previously been withdrawn from these operations in order to cover any Katangan escape routes from Stanleyville. An unknown number of Katangan troops were killed while they withdrew southward but the majority succeeded in moving via Punia to the area controlled by Jean Schramme and 10 Commando in Maniema. Schramme, who acted as a facilitator between the Katangans and the government, obtained an amnesty for the Katangans and they finally surrendered. The Katangan officers were then transported to prison in Elisabethville where the terms of the amnesty were ignored and they were executed. The first rebellion had failed and the end of 1966 saw President Mobutu consolidating his power, secure in the loyalty of 5 Commando and the ostensible support of 6 and 10 Commandos.

The Mercenary Rebellion

Jerry Puren now attempted to stage a second rebellion to reinstall Tshombe and, in the absence of any other willing or trustworthy mercenaries, selected Jean Schramme as the candidate to lead the rebellion. Jean Schramme, a planter who had lived and farmed in the Congo for decades had never ceased to support Tshombe and had established a virtual state within a state in the Maniema area in and around Punia, supported by his 10 Commando. During a meeting between Schramme, Denard and President Mobutu in December 1966 the latter made it clear that Schramme's Kansimba unit would be disbanded and replaced by ANC recruits loyal to Mobutu. In May 1967 Denard received instructions from Mobutu to disarm the Kansimbas in 10 Commando, a task he delayed until such time as he had visited Schramme at the latter's plantation in Yumbi, on the Lowa river north of Punia.

In June 1967 Denard visited Schramme again and the two mercenaries agreed on a coordinated revolt to oust President Mobutu. The plan called for Schramme and 10 Commando to advance from Yumbi and take Stanleyville, whereafter Denard's 100-odd 6 Commando mercenaries and 800 Katangans would join him. At the same time two of Schramme's officers, Noel and Hendricks, would each lead a 10 Commando column and take Bukavu and Kindu respectively. Schramme and Noel would then regroup at Yumbi before moving south to join Michel in Kindu where 10 Commando's new base would be established. Denard would hold Stanleyville and the northeast of the Congo. During the second phase of the operation Schramme and his force would rendezvous with approximately 2,000 former Katangan gendarmes and assault the strategic air base at Kamina in Katanga.

Members of 5 Commando bring an 81mm mortar into action. *Source*: James MacKenzie collection

Members of 52 Commando on the water. *Source*: James MacKenzie collection

5 Commando patrol. *Source*: James MacKenzie collection

Moise Tshombe would be flown to the base from exile in Spain which would lead to an uprising in the Katanga and Kasai provinces. The rebel cause would then demand the abdication of President Mobutu.

In an effort to increase the credibility of the plan, Jerry Puren and a group of fewer than ten mercenaries landed in Punia in a DC-4 piloted by Jack Malloch during the last week of June and unloaded arms and ammunition that they had picked up in Angola. On 1 July, however, Moise Tshombe's plane was hijacked while flying between Ibiza and Majorca off the coast of Spain and flown to Algeria where he was imprisoned and from where his death in prison would be announced two years later.

Early in July 1967 Denard contacted Schramme and at a subsequent meeting, informed the latter that 3 Paratroop Battalion (ANC) was due to arrive in Stanleyville by river within two days and Denard's orders to disarm 10 Commando would have to be carried out thereafter. The two commanders then decided to carry out the rebellion immediately.

On 5 July Schramme's 10 Commando launched surprise attacks on Stanleyville, Bukavu and Kindu as planned. Camp Ketele, the main objective in Stanleyville, was taken without any difficulty but the promised support from 6 Commando in the city was not forthcoming. In addition, 6 Commando's vehicles were concentrated in Stanleyville, while the troops were deployed outside the town as far as 100 kilometres away, leading to speculation that Denard was planning to embus 3 Paratroop Battalion and attack Schramme. Denard did, however, gather his dispersed troops over the next few days and, on returning

to Stanleyville, was wounded in the leg and evacuated by DC-3 aircraft to Rhodesia on 10 July.

Noel's column took Bukavu without any difficulty, but at Kindu the detachment under Michel Hendricks was driven back to the airport by the ANC battalion stationed there and they were forced to escape through the bush back to Yumbi. In Bukavu, the mercenary force consolidated its position, only to withdraw from the town after receiving a confusing radio message from Stanleyville directing them to return to Punia. After news of the fighting in Stanleyville reached Leopoldville, the 30-odd 6 Commando mercenaries working in mostly administrative and security positions in Kinshasa were rounded up by President Mobutu and shot out of hand.

On 12 July 1967 Schramme and his force withdrew from Stanleyville and, despite radio announcements that the Rwandan border had been sealed off by ANC battalions, he arrived in Bukavu three weeks later with a force of 1,100 men and 1,500 women and children and took the town with ease. The ANC troops fled across the Ruzizi river into Rwanda, handing in their weapons at the border as they crossed. By this time the 2,000-odd European civilians in the town had also fled across the border to Rwanda.

After settling in and establishing a defensive perimeter based on eight strongpoints on the high ground surrounding the town, Schramme indicated that he would negotiate with the government for a period of ten days, whereupon he would commence an advance on Katanga or even Leopoldville. This ultimatum was reciprocated by President Mobutu five days later, giving Schramme and his force

Members of 5 Commando rehearse seaborne landings at Baraka, 1966. *Source*: James MacKenzie collection

Rebels under ANC guard. *Source*: James MacKenzie collection

ten days to leave Bukavu. A spate of ultimatums and threats were traded back and forth between the two opponents over the 12-week period that Schramme held Bukavu. In mid October, after eight weeks of the siege, it was evident that the status quo was not likely to change in the near future.

In the interim Bob Denard had been released from hospital in Salisbury and returned to Angola from where he was in radio contact with Schramme on a daily basis. An attempt to obtain the services of a new political figurehead with which to effect a change of government in the Congo was now attempted by Denard. Such a person was Godfried Munongo, Tshombe's former minister of interior in the Katangan secession government. Munongo was imprisoned on the prison island at the mouth of the Congo river and on the night of 28 October a group of 13 mercenaries set about crossing the Congo river from Angola in canoes in a bid to free him. A force of 110 mercenaries and 50 Katangans had also been assembled on the Angola–Congo border in anticipation of his release. The intent was that once Munungo was freed, the force would advance into Katanga, open a Katangan front and support Munungo's political agenda. The raid was a dismal failure.

Strengthened by their success during the prison raid, the ANC launched an offensive against Bukavu with 7 and 9 Commandos and 2 and 3 Paratroop Battalions (ANC) on 29 October. After two days the exhausted ANC forces withdrew, thwarted by Schramme's judicial use of indirect fire and the mobility of the jeeps which brought machine-gun fire to bear at the correct place at the correct time.

On 1 November Denard's invasion force crossed the Angolan border into Katanga on bicycles and seized the village of Luashi, whereupon a section of the force pedalled to the manganese mining town of Kisenge, routed the ANC platoon and seized six cargo vehicles and two jeeps. Denard moved his operational headquarters north to Kasagi on the main route and railway line between Kolwezi and Dilolo the next day. Thousands of Katangans flocked into the deserted town in support of the mercenaries and a requirement for weapons and ammunition developed. The force allocated to obtain the weapons and ammunition advanced on Dilolo but withdrew to Kisenge after a series of air attacks and

ANC ambushes. With internal dissent rife, the force withdrew and crossed the Angolan border by 4 November. The second front had collapsed.

Bukavu Falls

Encouraged by their success in Katanga, the ANC attacked Bukavu along two axes. The greatest vulnerability of Schramme's forces—his lack of ammunition—enabled the southern axis of the ANC attack to penetrate the outer defensive perimeter, forcing 10 Commando to withdraw and decrease the size of the defensive perimeter. On 5 November Jean Schramme, together with 150 mercenaries, 800-odd Katangan soldiers and 1,500 women and children, withdrew across the Shangugu bridge to Rwanda and were disarmed and interned by Rwandan authorities at Shangugu. After a brief internment at Shangugu, the Katangan gendarmes and their camp followers were loaded aboard cargo vehicles and transported back into the Congo where, in spite of President Mobutu's promise of an amnesty, many, if not all were killed. The mercenaries remained in captivity for six months before being released and flown back to Europe. The mercenary revolt had collapsed.

CHAPTER NINE:
CONCLUSION

This discourse is aimed at contributing towards the provision of some lucidity on the military dimension of the events that shook the Congo during the 1960s; a number of startling events were indeed unveiled.

Who would believe that a country that provided the uranium for the first atomic bombs and that housed one of only three nuclear research facilities in Africa would also use soldiers who, through the power of superstition and a few machetes, could conquer swathes of territory as large as any European state?

Who would believe that the United States would be party to a conflict where the USAF flew over 2,000 missions and covered in excess of 40 million kilometres while supporting soldiers ranged against a NATO ally in the Congo? Who would believe that the United States would then partner with that same NATO ally in the Congo a year later to conduct one of the most audacious joint airborne operations in Africa?

Who would believe that the Katangan secession would witness the death of a UN secretary-general and the bankrupting of the organization? Who would believe that the deaths of Patrice Lumumba and of Moise Tshombe were due to natural causes?

Who would believe that in a far-flung country such as the Congo, British and European citizens seconded to the United Nations would fight British and European citizens seconded to Katangan units? Who would believe that mercenary air forces

could be mobilized overnight, that Che Guevara fought and failed in the Congo, that Cubans actually fought Cubans in the Congo and that a recent president of the country was once a junior partner in a struggling insurgency?

Who would believe that Belgian navy minesweepers provided naval gunnery support fire during a pitched battle and lost the battle in the Congo, that mercenaries were universally regarded as the saviours of hundreds of hostages at one time in the conflict, only to be branded as criminals a few years later? Who would believe that the Congo was indeed invaded by a force of 100 men on bicycles?

At independence in 1960 the Republic of the Congo embarked on a journey that was untidy, convoluted and often without any causal relationship between events. The characteristics of this rich expanse of Africa and subsequent events did not necessarily weave together to form a single golden thread on political or military levels that serve to anchor what happened over the first decade of its independence. Clarity is not in the nature of the Congo story.

In Africa there are examples of military conflicts in which the belligerents and their actions are such that one cannot but conclude, without fear of contradiction, that the truth is indeed stranger than fiction. The military operations undertaken during and after the transition of the Congo, from colony to independent state, undoubtedly fall within this category.

Sources and Bibliography

Chapter 1. The following publications were consulted during the compilation of this chapter: Arnold, G. & Weiss, R. *Strategic Highways of Africa*. Julian Friedman Publishers, 1977; Chakravorty, B. *The Congo Operation, 1960–63*. Ministry of Defence, New Delhi, 1974; Merriam, A. P. *Congo: Background to Conflict*. Northwest University Press, 1961; Moorcroft, P. *African Nemesis: War and Revolution in Southern Africa, 1945–2010*. Brasseys, London, 2010; US Foreign Relations, 1952–1954, Volume XI, *Belgian Congo: Matters of Concern to the United States in the Belgian Congo*, 511.55a/2-354; www.country-data.com.

Chapter 2. The following people were interviewed and publications consulted during the compilation of this chapter: Interviews: M. Neyt, September 2011. Publications: Chakravorty, B. *The Congo Operation, 1960–63.* Ministry of Defence, New Delhi, 1974; Clarke, S.J.G. *The Congo Mercenary: A History and Analysis*. The South African Institute of International Affairs, 1968; Merriam, A. P. *Congo: Background to Conflict*. Northwest University Press, 1961; Van Nederveen, G. K. *USAF Airlift into the Heart of Darkness, the Congo 1960–1978*. Airpower Research Institute, Maxwell Air Force Base, AL, 2001; *VTB* Magazine, Het Driemaandelijkse Bulletin van de 'Vieilles Tiges' van de Belgische Luchtvaart, No 3-2011; www.country-data.com.

Chapter 3. The following publications were consulted during the compilation of this chapter: Archer, J. *Congo: The Birth of a New Nation*. Bailey Brothers & Swinfen Limited, Folkstone, 1970; Calder, R. *Agony of the Congo*. Victor Gallancz, London, 1961; Merriam. A. P. *Congo: Background to Conflict*. Northwest University Press, 1961; U.S. State Department. *Central Files on the Congo 1960–1963*. National Archives of the United States, Washington.

Chapter 4. The following publications were consulted during the compilation of this chapter: Calder, R. *Agony of the Congo*. Victor Gallancz, London, 1961; Diosso, O. *La Mutinerie de la Force Publique, le 5 Juillet 1960.* www.lepotentiel.com; Lawson, R. *Strange Soldiering*. Hodder & Stroughton, 1963; Merriam. A. P. *Congo: Background to Conflict*. Northwest University Press, 1961; Pitta, R. *UN Forces 1948–94*. Osprey Military Elite Series No. 54. London, 1994; Sonck, J.P. *Les Opérations au Congo*. www.congo-1960.be; Salt, B. *A Pride of Eagles: The Definitive History of the Rhodesian Air Force 1920–1980*. Covos Day, Johannesburg, 2001; Van Nederveen, G. K. *USAF Airlift into the Heart of Darkness, the Congo 1960–1978*. Airpower Research Institute, Maxwell Air Force Base, AL, 2001.

Chapter 5. The following publications were consulted during the compilation of this chapter: Chakravorty, B. *The Congo Operation, 1960–63.* Ministry of Defence, New Delhi, 1974; Gérard-Libois, J. *Katanga Secession*. The University of Wisconsin Press, 1966; Hoare. M. *The Road to Kalamata: A Congo Mercenary's Personal Memoire*. Paladin Press, 2010; http://navysite.de/cruisebooks; O'Donoghue, D. *The Irish Army in the Congo 1960–1964*. Irish Academic Press, 2006; Puren, J. as told to Pottinger, B. *Mercenary Commander*. Galago, Alberton, 1986; Schramme, J. *Le Bataillon Léopard: Souvenirs d'un Africain Blanc*. Robert Laffont, 1969; Sitkowski, A. *UN Peacekeeping: Myth and Reality*. Praeger Security International, 2006; Thomas, G. S. *Mercenary Troops in Modern Africa*. Westview Press, 1984; United Nations Security Council, *Report to the Secretary-General … the Interrogation of Thirty Mercenaries Apprehended in Kabalo on 7 April 1961*. Report S/4790, 14 April 1961; Van Nederveen, G. K. *USAF Airlift into the Heart of Darkness, the Congo 1960–1978*. Airpower Research Institute, Maxwell Air Force Base, AL, 2001; Von Horn, C. *Soldiering for Peace*. Cassel, 1966; Zumbach, J. *On Wings of War: My Life as a Pilot Adventurer*. André Deutsch, 1975.

Chapter 6. The following people were interviewed and publications consulted during the compilation of this chapter: Interviews: M. Neyt, J.P. Sonck. Publications: Clarke, S.J.G. *The Congo Mercenary: A History and Analysis*. The South African Institute of International Affairs, Johannesburg, 1968; Closset, A. *Les Compagnons de L'Ommegang*. Les Editions de l'Aronde, 1995; Derolez, S.B.H (ed). *Red & Black Dragon, Ommegang, 2004*. Defence Printing House, 2004; Dodenhoff, G.H. *The Congo: A Case Study of Mercenary Employment*. Naval War College Review; Germani, H. *White Soldiers in Black Africa*. Nasionale Boekhandel, Cape Town, 1967; Glasgow, W.H. *Operations Dragon Rouge and Dragon Noir*. HQ US Army, Europe, Operations Division, Historical Section, 1965; Gleijeses, P. *"Flee! The White Giants Are Coming!" The United States, the Mercenaries, and the Congo, 1964–65*. Diplomatic History, Spring 1994; Hingston, M. *Renegade Hero*. Pen & Sword Aviation, Barnsley, 2011; Hoare, M. *Congo Mercenary*. Robert Hale, London, 1969; Johnson, R.C. *Heart of Darkness: The Tragedy of the Congo, 1960–67*. 1997, www.worldatwar.net, accessed 12 June 2011; Northom, P. *Dans Stanleyville*. Editions Masoin, Brussels, 2011; Odom, T.P. *Dragon Operations: Hostage Rescues in the Congo, 1964–1965*. Levenworth Papers Number 14, Combat Studies Institute, Fort Levenworth, Kansas, 1988; Puren. J. as told to Pottinger, B. *Mercenary Commander*. Galago, Alberton, 1986; Reed, D. *111 Days in Stanleyville*. Harper & Row, New York. 1965; Schramme, J. *Le Bataillon Léopard: Souvenirs d'un Africain Blanc*. Robert Laffont, 1969; Thomas, G. S. *Mercenary Troops in Modern Africa*. Westview Press, 1984; Vandewalle, E.R. *L'Ommegang: Odyssée et Reconquête de Stanleyville, 1964*. Le Livre Africain, Collection Temoinage Africain, Brussels, 1970; Van Nederveen, G. K. *USAF Airlift into the Heart of Darkness, the Congo 1960–1978*. Airpower Research Institute, Maxwell Air Force Base, AL, 2001; Wagoner, F.E.

Andrew Hudson majored in military history at the South Africa Military Academy; after two decades as an infantry officer in the South African Defence Force, ten of which were spent in the operational areas, he moved into the private sector. Still a soldier at heart he divides his time between earning an income, indulging his passion for collecting books on conflict in Africa, and road-running in weird and wonderful locations. He is co-author of *Four Ball, One Tracer: Commanding Executive Outcomes in Angola and Sierra Leone* (June 2012).

For Dee, as always,
and for soldiers within whose souls
the warrior spirit is kindled

A special word of thanks and acknowledgement to Michal Neyt without whose assistance this project would have been virtually impossible. I salute you, an old African soldier like me, for your tireless efforts, hospitality and for introducing me to the virtues of distilled Normandy apples. To Luc Marchal, another African soldier, I thank you with respect. Thank you to Dirk Doms and Jempy Bonjean, at the Military Archives in Brussels, for opening the files and my eyes. To J.P. Sonck, thank you for the pictures, our discussions in Brussels and the benefit of your expert knowledge thereafter.

Thanks are also due to Alf Blume for recovering a set of photographs taken by an unknown ONUC soldier, from a refuse bin; and to Daniel Brackx for the aircraft images and the encouragement. Thank you also, Jean-Luc Ernst, for the images and your very informative website at www.stanleyville.be.

A special debt of gratitude is also due to James Mackenzie, my collector friend of more than two decades, for assisting with photographs and for sharing his vast knowledge. Thank you also to Iain Peddle, for your unique and valuable insights into naval warfare on Lake Tanganyika. Also to Martin and Cilla van Oppen for opening your home and your attic papers to me.

And to Angela Thomas at the South African Institute of International Affairs, thank you for restoring my faith in excellence in the field of information research. Thank you also to Patricia Laloum for the translation work.

Finally, a profound and special word of thanks and appreciation to Kim Zimmerman for the excellent, tireless work at converting scrawled lines on a piece of paper into such colourful and informative maps. This is our second collaboration and I look forward to your talented inputs for many more.

Sources and Bibliography *continued ...*

Dragon Rouge: The Rescue of Hostages in the Congo. National Defence University, Washington, 1980, reprinted 2011.

Chapter 7: The following people were interviewed and publications consulted during the compilation of this chapter: Interviews: M. Neyt, I. Peddle, J.P. Sonck. Primary documents and publications: Baker, C. *Wild Goose: The Life and Times of Hugh van Oppen.* Mpemba Books, Cardiff, 2002; Clarke, S.J.G. *The Congo Mercenary: A History and Analysis.* The South African Institute of International Affairs, Johannesburg, 1968; Closset, A. *Les Compagnons de L'Ommegang.* Les Editions de l'Aronde, 1995; Germani, H. *White Soldiers in Black Africa.* Nasionale Boekhandel, Cape Town, 1967; Gleijeses, P. *"Flee! The White Giants Are Coming!" The United States, the Mercenaries, and the Congo, 1964–65.* Diplomatic History, Spring, 1994; Headquarters 5 Commando. *Operation Banzi* (M. Hoare's written orders for Operation Banzi). Albertville, 25 September 1965; Headquarters Operation South (Sud). *Ordre d'Operation No 1.* No date, signed by Lieutenant-Colonel Hardenne, Chief of Staff, Operation Sud on behalf of Colonel Kakudji, Officer Commanding Operation Sud; Hoare, M. *Congo Warriors.* Paladin Press, Boulder, 1991; Peddle, I. *Congo Experiences.* Unpublished. 15 November 2011; Reed, D. *111 Days in Stanleyville.* Harper & Row, New York. 1965; Rogers, A. *Someone Else's War: Mercenaries from 1960 to the Present.* HarperCollins Publishers, London, 1998; Sonck, J.P. *Quand les Maquis de Kabila Menaçaient Albertville.* www.albertville.stools.net accessed 26 March 2012; Taibo, P.I. *Guevara, Also Known as Che.* St Martin's Press, New York, 1997; Thomas, G. S. *Mercenary Troops in Modern Africa.* Westview Press, 1984; Vandewalle, E.R. *L'Ommegang: Odyssée et Reconquête de Stanleyville, 1964.* Le Livre Africain, Collection Temoinage Africain, Brussels, 1970; Van Nederveen, G. K. *USAF Airlift into the Heart of Darkness, the Congo 1960–1978.* Airpower Research Institute, Maxwell Air Force Base, AL, 2001; Villafaña, F.R. *Cold War in the Congo: The Confrontation of Cuban Military Forces, 1960–1967.* Transaction Publishers, New Brunswick, 2009.

Chapter 8: The following publications were consulted during the compilation of this chapter: Clarke, S.J.G. *The Congo Mercenary: A History and Analysis.* The South African Institute of International Affairs, Johannesburg, 1968; Honorin, M. *La Fin des Mercenaires, Bukavu, Novembre, 1967.* Robert Laffont, Paris 1968; Mockler, A. *The New Mercenaries.* Corgi Books. 1986; Puren, J. as told to Pottinger, B. *Mercenary Commander.* Galago, Alberton, 1986; Rogers, A. *Someone Else's War: Mercenaries from 1960 to the Present.* HarperCollins Publishers, London, 1998; Schramme, J. *Le Bataillon Léopard: Souvenirs d'un Africain Blanc.* Robert Laffont, Paris 1969.